TIME ON THE BOARDS
26,000 Performances over 60 Years

A Ventriloquist's Memoir
by Sammy King

Foreword by Jay Johnson

This book is dedicated to everyone who has ever found the courage to walk out on stage.

Special thanks to my cousin, Rhonda Faden Portnoy, for putting my thoughts into words.

Praise for Sammy King

"Sammy King is a great ventriloquial technician, and his commitment to character is wonderful." – Edgar Bergen, 1968

"As I sat in the audience of the Palm Springs Follies and watched Sammy King on stage, I marveled at his talent, his technique, and his obviously considerable time on the boards." – Paul Winchell, 2002

"I have been a friend and fan of Sammy King for longer than either he or I will admit. He sets a new mark for all ventriloquists to reach every time he walks on stage. Thanks for showing us all how, Sammy." – Jay Johnson

"Sammy King has been an icon in the ventriloquial world for many years. His lectures and coaching have helped many aspiring ventriloquists who are just starting out or need improvement in their performances. Personally, I have enjoyed watching Sammy perform over the years and rate him among the top vents of recent decades." – Jimmy Nelson

"Sammy King has always been a great inspiration in my career." – Jeff Dunham

"Sammy King is the ventriloquist I watched when I was a kid." – Ronn Lucas

"When I started performing, my mentor became Sammy King because his influence directed me into becoming a performer and not just a vent. I give him credit for influencing me in how to put together a professional act." – Brad Cummings

"The word I would use to sum up Sammy King's act is AWESOME! He is fast, funny, original and a complete show-stopper whenever he is on the bill. I couldn't recommend any act any higher than Sammy's!" – Mark Wade, Executive Director, Vent Haven International Ventriloquist Con-VENTion

"King" of Ventriloquists Returns to Follies Stage

Sammy King and Francisco

You asked for a return engagement by ventriloquist extraordinaire Sammy King, 62, and his wiseacre partner "Francisco," and the Follies obliged!

Born in Brownsville, Texas, he began his career after seeing mentor Paul Winchell (a Palm Springs resident) on television. "I sat my kid brother on my knee and squeezed the back of his neck to cue the 'dummy'," says King.

Since 1958, he has given over 25,000 performances including the very last Ed Sullivan Show. He played the Crazy Horse Saloon in Paris for ten years, appeared in ten major Las Vegas production shows, and has opened for Rich Little, Bill Cosby, Cher, Ray Charles and Tony Bennett.

"My most memorable performances were in Viet Nam for the USO and performing at the 100th birthday party of legendary ventriloquist Señor Wences in Las Vegas," remembers King.

Variety Newspaper calls King, "...the KING of Ventriloquists" and desert resident Merv Griffin says, "...(the) funniest act I've seen in years."

Contents

Jay Johnson

Foreword

Being Sammy King
by Jay Johnson

Sammy King is an excellent ventriloquist, accomplished musician, brilliant entertainer, puppeteer, puppet maker, inspired teacher, artist, and performing coach. More important: he is also my friend. We have more in common than just being ventriloquists from Texas. As random as it may sound, Texas has produced more than its share of notable ventriloquists. To name a few in alphabetical order: Jeff Dunham, Terry Fator, Jay Johnson, Sammy King, and Ronn Lucas. Even before I knew he was from Texas, my torchbearer was Sammy King. I became his fan while in my teens. He mixed music with ventriloquism, playing flamenco guitar while throwing his voice. It was this combination of art forms that fascinated me. That's what I wanted to do. As much as I tried, however, I realized at 19 years old, I would never BE Sammy King.

I was performing my ventriloquist act during summer break from college at AstroWorld (a Houston theme park, now long gone, as are any more mentions of Texas). One of the girl singers in my show at the Crystal Palace asked if I knew a ventriloquist named Sammy King? Of course, I knew Sammy King – not personally, but I was a big fan. I had seen him on *The Merv Griffin Show* and live at the Adolphus Hotel Kings Club in Dallas, Texas. My Dad had taken me to the nightclub specifically to see Sammy's unique vent act when I was in my mid-teens. At the time, I thought it was called the Kings Club because Sammy owned it. So, I said to the AstroWorld singer, "I know Sammy… *Why?*" She said, "He's a friend of mine. He's coming to see our show today." I felt a special kind of nerves that day. Knowing a famous ventriloquist was in the audience was an experience I never had before.

After a joke in my act, Squeaky "outed me" to Sammy. From the stage, he said, "You stole that from Sammy King." Even my wooden partner knew I wasn't Sammy King. But, we met and became friends, nonetheless. Our paths would cross again later. Sammy called me to ask if I could sub for him in John Daniels' *Shazam* show at the Carillon Hotel in Miami. He needed a week off, and the show needed a ventriloquist to fill the spot in his absence. Sammy liked my act from AstroWorld and recommended me to John Daniel, who hired me, sight unseen on Sammy's word alone. I jumped at the chance; it was a dream come true. I would actually get to be Sammy King for a week. *Shazam* was a magic revue at the Carillon Hotel showroom featuring John Daniels' magic assisted by eight sexy female dancers. My experience as a 19-year-old Sammy King went something like this: I lived in a small hotel room on Miami Beach. It was a snowbird retreat. I was 40 years younger than anyone registered there.

I left for work each evening as the rapidly-aging residents migrated to their pool chairs at the front of the Ocean Surf Motel. Dressed and ready, I stood at the entrance of the motel waiting for my ride to the theater.

Soon, Bunny and Sondra, both showgirl dancers, one blond and one brunette, would arrive in a Corvette convertible, looking fabulous. Both were in the show and gave me a ride to the hotel each night. Everyone at the pool bar watched as a college kid, in a dark suit, tossed a black case into the back of a powder blue vet and climbed into the front seat with two hot babes and drive off down Ocean Avenue. I soon became the talk of the Ocean Surf Motel.

After several evenings of watching this routine, one elderly man yelled from the bar, "What is it that you do every night, son?" I said, "Ventriloquism, sir." He looked at me, my black case, the two babes, the corvette, and burst out laughing, "That's a good one!" he yelled back. Yep, it's good to be "the King."

Hubris soon takes over. I am a spring break college kid who has hit the jackpot. Every night I am backstage with a bevy of beautiful dancers who wear very little clothing on stage and much less off stage. With high hopes of hitting a home run, I finally get the courage to say to one of the cutest dancers, "Have you ever been ravaged by a sexy ventriloquist." With the delivery of a Burlesque stripper, she replied, "Not since Sammy left." I crash and burn realizing, once and for all, I am not Sammy King. I am so glad Sammy wrote this autobiography, so we can remember his talents for years to come. His career, with over 26,000 performances all around the world, is a singularity in the world of show business. His is the modern day story of a traveling vaudevillian, recounting times only recently past, but never to be seen again. With the perspective of a lifetime, the truth has always been evident: there is only one Sammy King, and there will never be another like him.

Author's Note

The purpose of writing my performance history is to share my love of the stage in hopes of inspiring others to do the same. Throughout my career, I have committed myself to this goal – not only for ventriloquists, but for all types of entertainers, because talent is both a gift and a responsibility to be shared with the world.

I have often been asked for words of wisdom based on my experiences. I want to make it clear that experience is not based on how many years one has been performing. It has more to do with the number of performances. So, when someone tells me they have "been in show business," or performing, for 20 years, I usually ask how often they were on stage. The answer I usually get is "just about every weekend." To me, that says about two shows a week with five days off in-between. At best, that amounts to about 100 shows a year for 20 years. All downtime adds stage rust, so growth and fine tuning is rather limited. The great vaudevillians of years gone by did six to eight shows a day and usually worked 50 weeks a year, so that meant a lot of polish and fine tuning.

Time on the Boards is what I remember of my history on stage, almost 26,000 performances over a period of more than 60 years. While not at a vaudevillian's pace, it is considerably more than the experience most performers of today are generally getting under their proverbial belts. Once becoming a celebrity, or star, few entertainers work 10 to 12 shows a week, 50 weeks a year.

I feel that it has been a divine blessing to have lived my life on stages all over the world and to have given a few folks moments of entertainment, joy, and laughter. It has been most gratifying and certainly rewarding, but the real reward was not monetary; it was always simply the applause.

-- *Sammy*

Introduction

The title of my story comes from a simple statement conveyed to me by Paul Winchell, who, in my opinion, was the world's greatest ventriloquist of the 20th century. It happened the first time I performed without realizing Dr. Winchell was in the audience, and it took place at the Plaza Theatre in Palm Springs, California, during a season with the Fabulous Palm Springs Follies in 2002.

The policy of the Palm Springs Follies stated that whenever a V.I.P. was in the audience, no one in the cast was to be told. I suppose the reasoning was that it could possibly hinder one's performance, either by adding nervous energy, adrenaline, or making cast members try a little too hard, which could actually have a negative effect. So, just prior to each finale, the managing director and master of ceremonies, Riff Markowitz, was given cards used to announce the names of all groups and celebrities in attendance. At this particular show, Paul Winchell was in the audience, and, as his presence was announced, I was in my dressing room listening to the show on the monitor. I quickly tried to remember the audience reaction to my act that evening.

After each show, cast members met the audience as they exited through the lobby for the traditional "meet and greet." As I first came face to face with Paul Winchell, he stuck out his hand, which I shook gently, so as not to hurt the seemingly fragile, aging, bearded man who had been my childhood idol. I noticed a rather odd look in his eyes, and, through the thick glasses, I could tell he was flashing back to a time when all the great acts of vaudevillian days recalled the thousands of shows it took to perfect an act. He looked at me and simply sighed, shook his head, and said, "Time on the Boards," obviously understanding how much of my life it had taken to do what he had just seen on stage (at that point, almost 25,000 entrances and exits). It was not necessarily a compliment, just a simple fact.

Ten years earlier, in the 1990s, I had performed my act knowing Dr. Winchell was in the house. It took place at the First International Ventriloquist Convention in Las Vegas, Nevada, at the Judy Bailey Theatre on the campus of the University of Nevada, Las Vegas, with hundreds of ventriloquists in the audience. On the closing night's show, I shared the stage with a number of other professional "vents." In order to do the very best performance possible, I had hired four Mariachi's to play the music to my act with Francisco, the Mexican parrot. I also did a two-minute bit with "Teddy," played by a 40-pound dwarf named Kevin Brown. (Kevin's father, Johnny Brown, was one of the Lollipop Guild trio from the film, *The Wizard of Oz*.) For the act, Teddy wore a mask resembling a ventriloquial figure, with a mouth movement I controlled by a cable that ran around his neck to the middle of his back. The routine finished with the singing of "Old McDonald had a Farm," Teddy jumping off the stool, taking a bow, and running off stage. After that show, Ronn Lucas offered to buy the mask idea from me, but I simply said he could have it for free.

It was the day after that last show that I received a phone call from ventriloquist, Jerry Layne, who had accompanied Dr. Winchell on the trip to Las Vegas, asking, "Do you want to hear what Paul Winchell said about you?" Before I could answer "no," he went on to tell me that "Winch" had said, "...all those guys like Ronn and Jeff...they're really good, but, that Sammy King, he's 'The One'." Well, if my life had ended then and there, I could have died a very happy man! But, my life did not end right then. There were more unexpected turns in my career yet to come, and they would change everything.

Life on stage (as I knew it) actually ended some years later, when I slipped into something comfortable – a coma. It was Independence Day weekend, 2008, and I had finished a three-month Christmas show with Andy Williams in Branson, Missouri, followed by a tour of various cities in America. I decided to stay in Branson with Clay Cooper's show at the Caravel Theatre. But, for some reason I don't recall, the theater was dark that holiday weekend, and I went down to Texas for a couple of days. (Francisco stayed in Missouri.) While visiting with about 20 relatives and circus folks in Houston and enjoying a homemade Mexican dinner of tamales and cabrito (kid goat), I had a massive heart attack. I do not remember anything after the ambulance trip to the hospital. During my unconscious state over the next three months, or so, I was restrained at the wrists and ankles and on life support. It was then that I began recalling, in vivid images, the thousands of trips I had made to the stage during my 50+ years of shows and all my "Time on the Boards."

When I finally opened my eyes for the first time since that ambulance ride, I could neither speak nor move. I could only listen while I was told what had happened to me and what to expect for my future. The prognosis was not good. I cried a lot and for a long time. Being intubated for three months had permanently scarred 60% of my vocal cords and the heart attack had left only 25% of my heart functional. With tracheal stenosis (a breathing tube in my neck), and what was left of my heart, I would probably never be able to speak the same as before – not good news for a ventriloquist! At the time, I didn't think anything could be worse…until later, when I was told I had cancer.

And, so, my history of *Time on the Boards* begins….

The Beginning
The 1940s

Sammy King - 1946

Ventriloquism began for me in 1949 while listening to *The Edgar Bergen and Charlie McCarthy Show* on the radio. I can remember many things about that time because it was certain that I did not live like other children my age. I was a very quiet, shy, and introverted little dreamer. All I knew for sure was that I went to bed every night to the sounds of lions, tigers, and bears, along with monkeys, elephants and various other wild animals from different parts of the world. That may sound like a tale of dreams, but, in fact, no part of this story is untrue, imagined, or made up in any way. Everything actually happened to me exactly as I remember it, though I often went to sleep wishing I would wake up living in a rather normal neighborhood with a mom and dad, a brother, two sisters, and, maybe, even a cocker spaniel in the yard. But, that life was not to be – not for me, Sammy King.

Our family home was located in the middle of "Snakeville," as it was called ("La Vivoreria" in Spanish). The house belonged to my grandfather, William Abraham Lieberman, known to the world as "Snake King." Papito, as we children called him, was a Polish immigrant who had run away from his home in New York as a young teenager in the 1880s to join the circus. In those days, travel was by horse and wagon, and circus folk were no different. So, Papito's adventurous gypsy-like life eventually led him south and west across America until he reached Brownsville, Texas, where the Rio Grande River empties into the Gulf of Mexico.

Snake King

Part of my grandfather's circus side show was a snake exhibit, and South Texas had a lot of rattlesnakes just "for the catching." So, his name change was a result of the title given him for catching and selling western diamondback rattlesnakes, a skill Papito learned from a carnival showman who befriended him as a young man. This practice and a good

1

head for business eventually made Snake King the world's largest importer and exporter of snakes, wild animals, and birds, including thousands of Mexican parrots.

The Snake King with cages of imported Mexican parrots and macaws

By the time I, Samuel Leon, was born to David Faden and Pauline King Faden at the Fort Brown Army Hospital in Brownsville, Texas, on September 25, 1940, the huge animal complex of Snakeville was crawling with hundreds of birds, animals, and reptiles, which were eventually sent to either zoos, pet shops, circuses, individuals, or companies that had various uses for them.

My uncle, Manuel King, had been known as the world's youngest lion tamer in 1934 at age 12, and my grandfather promoted him with that billing for performing in arenas, circuses, and fairs from the Steel Pier in

Uncle Manuel - The World's Youngest Lion Tamer

Atlantic City to extravaganzas in Mexico that drew large crowds and paid a lot of money. In 1936, Manuel King starred in a movie with the famous lion tamer, Clyde Beatty. The movie, *Darkest Africa*, was actually filmed in Brownsville and was later made into a cliff hanger series of chapters. By the time Manuel was too old to be billed as a boy lion tamer, the novelty had worn off, and my uncle joined the Army, returning to Brownsville only after Snake King left the country and took his money with him to live with his mistress in Mexico.

After his discharge from the Army, Uncle Manuel expanded the animal importing business, converting it to what was known as the Snake King Zoo. I was five years old at the time and starting first grade at Los Ebanos Elementary School, just down the dirt road from Snakeville. Walking to school every day, I passed the rows of caged African lions that had once been part of Uncle Manuel's act. And, while the family was very well known in the town of Brownsville, to me, it was no great honor to be a child who lived in a zoo.

The Snakeville office circa 1946

The only childhood entertainment I remember was either watching my Uncle Joe milking rattlesnakes for their venom, which was worth its weight in gold, or listening to an old radio show featuring Edgar Bergen, Charlie McCarthy, and Mortimer Snerd. One night, I clearly remember asking my mother if the voices on the radio were one man doing different characters. She surprisingly answered, "Yes, he's a ventriloquist." When I asked what that meant, my mother said, "That's someone who can talk without moving his lips. He has a little doll-like dummy that he makes talk by throwing his voice." It was an epiphany for me!

3

As I listened to the voices, I knew instinctively how one person could speak for two characters and how one could "become" two different characters at the same time. Ventriloquism was something I immediately knew I could do; however, there were no schools for this art in Brownsville, Texas, so I taught myself. I sat my younger brother, Morty, on my lap, and I would squeeze the back of his neck cueing his mouth to open and close as I would do his speaking without moving my lips. I named my new "partner" Teddy. The trouble with using Morty as my dummy was that he couldn't keep a straight face. When we'd get to a punch line, he'd be laughing and "talking" at the same time.

After a while, I moved on to a Charlie McCarthy replica dummy (also named Teddy) with a string that came out the back of the neck to move the mouth. It wasn't that I didn't like my dummy – he looked like Charlie McCarthy – but, I made a few changes to make him look unique. The following is our first script together:

Teddy: *Sam, I'm in the Army.*

Sammy: How'd you get in the Army?

Teddy: *I got drafted.*

Sammy: Drafted? Teddy, you're only 12.

Teddy: (Singing) *I tried to tell them I was too young.*

Okay, so it wasn't much, but I was only nine years old at the time.

My mother gave me a hand-carved, wooden ventriloquist dummy figure for my 13th birthday, and, of course, I also named him Teddy. As a Bar Mitzvah present from the Temple Beth El congregation, I spent that summer at Camp Young Judea near Center Point, Texas. I took Teddy with me and kept him under my bunk until the camp talent show. "We" had a five-minute routine of mostly borrowed material from all the great ventriloquists like Jimmy Nelson and Paul Winchell. Teddy, who was made in Mexico, had bushy eyebrows that moved by a separate control lever from the mouth. It was my first experience in operating head, mouth, and eyebrow movements on a dummy. The night of the camp talent show, I got the biggest laughs every time Teddy leaned out toward a girl in the audience and moved his eyebrows up and down. It was the beginning of learning to use attitude and character to get laughs instead of just jokes. I left Camp Young Judea with the "Most Talented Camper" certificate. It was the first award I ever received and a great confidence builder. I couldn't sleep much when I got back home, dreaming over and over about one day being in show business.

4

In 1952, television was the most important thing in the world to me, especially *The Ed Sullivan Show* on Sunday nights, because it often featured ventriloquists, and I knew them all – not personally, but their names and their acts. I continued to dream of one day appearing on that same show and earning the respect of all those great ventriloquists I was always watching. That was the beginning of my career and my dedication to ventriloquism.

The Early Years
The 1950s

I never slept soundly. My early nights brought a variety of sounds that could keep anyone awake and even induce nightmares. The constant sounds of African lions and other wild animals were not uncommon in that house in Snakeville.

"Chubby" Guilfoyle with Manuel King circa 1933

By the time I was 12 years old, my mother recognized my talents as a ventriloquist and thought it would be a great novelty to have her son perform with "talking" lions. She hired the same fellow who trained my uncle in his act to teach me lion taming and develop my "new" career. He was a thin old man named "Chubby" Guilfoyle, but it should have been "Lefty." He had lost an arm, (*even though he knew exactly where it was*), from a lion-taming incident. Good thinking, Mom…an old one-armed alcoholic is going to put me in a cage with African lions. I'm sure any 12-year-old would be okay with that scenario! And, to add her own flair for showmanship, my mother decided that a mixed group of lions and yummy-tasting goats would catapult the act to fame.

I spent three one-hour sessions in a cage with two six-month-old lion cubs and five just-weaned goats. But, when I didn't show much heart for the proposed act, my mother gave up on the idea. The lions were happy with the decision, and I don't know what happened with the goats, but I was sure the scar on my eyebrow from "Brownie" butting me would be my last. After all, I was already doing Edgar Bergen's act, with some changes to make it my own. At the time, I was also a big fan of *Kukla, Fran, and Ollie*, a television show featuring puppets, and that's when it occurred to me that I should include a parrot in my act. What could be more believable than to have a talking parrot puppet (instead of a real lion!)? But, there were no parrot puppets in my hometown, so, ultimately, it would be almost 10 more years before a version of Francisco was first "hatched."

6

The snowbirds migrated to Brownsville in travel trailers during the winter to get away from the cold weather up north. One Saturday night, my dummy, Teddy, and I appeared in a show at the Los Amigos Trailer Park where I had previously done my act with my brother, Morty, but this time, I got paid. The master of ceremonies, an old showman named Sy Nickum, introduced me by saying, "Here is a young man that you're going to see on *The Ed Sullivan Show* someday." Other than briefly wishing his words would come true for me, I didn't give the announcement a second thought. So, after the act, I passed the hat around the room and left with almost five dollars in change. I now considered myself a professional! And, ever since then, I have always viewed my act and the art of ventriloquism through the eyes of a professional. Although I only performed about 10 times a year during my school days, I practiced my act daily for hours, always alone and always in front of a mirror. I also started teaching myself to play the guitar. As I practiced playing the guitar more and more, I was excited to discover that I could play and do my ventriloquism at the same time.

At Cummings Junior High School in 1952, Teddy and I won first place in a talent contest, and I also wrote, directed, and starred in my first play – a spoof on the television show *Dragnet*. I called it *Drag a Net*, which I later changed to *Dragon Neck*. In the performance, I played Sergeant Thursday investigating a missing person. It was the first time I appeared on stage without Teddy, who, by the way, had changed in looks because I didn't like his eyes. They were glass eyes and looked too human, so I covered them with plaster and painted eyes that were more cartoon-like. During that same time, I also entered a drawing contest. Molten Ty Cobb had a children's television show down in the Rio Grande Valley, and, on one show, he invited viewers to enter a "blooper" contest. No one knew what a blooper was; the idea was to submit whatever one imagined. My entry was an alien-looking being with antennas on his head and a rattlesnake belt. I was glued to the television set when Mr. Cobb announced the winner, and I could see it was my drawing even before it was held in front of the camera. I won! If not for ventriloquism, I would definitely have been a cartoonist or a guitar player. I spent as much time with a guitar on my lap as with a dummy, and both drawing and music would always play important roles in developing my act.

The summer before my senior year in high school, I took a trip to Houston, 300 miles north of Brownsville. I rode there on a 3½ horsepower Cushman motor scooter with Teddy strapped behind me in a suitcase. The eight-hour journey ended when the engine threw its only rod. Stranded just outside of Richmond, Texas, I called my Uncle Manuel in Houston, and, a couple of hours later, we finally drove into Houston with the scooter in the back of his Volkswagen bus/truck.

I had once visited the big city of Houston with my sister, Libby, on a Young Judea convention when I was 15. The convention was at the Shamrock Hotel and included a talent contest, in which I won first place. I remembered the Shamrock Hotel as a place so impressive that I vowed one day to return. After my Uncle Manuel and I arrived at our destination, we settled in and wrote the following new script for my act:

Sammy: We're here to entertain these people, so tell them about yourself.
Teddy: *Like what?*
Sammy: Where do you live?
Teddy: *In that suitcase.*
Sammy: And your parents?
Teddy: *No, there's not enough room in there for them.*
Sammy: No, I mean, like, what do they do?
Teddy: *At night or during the day?*
Sammy: I mean what do they do for a living?
Teddy: *They're in the metal business.*
Sammy: The metal business?
Teddy: *Yeah, my mother irons and my father steals.*
Sammy: That's not funny.
Teddy: *Well, then, let's talk about YOUR family, they're VERY funny.*
Sammy: My family is really something.
Teddy: *You said it.*
Sammy: I mean my family amounts to something. I've got an uncle in oil.
Teddy: *That's nothing; I've got a cousin in plywood.*
Sammy: And, my sister, Libby Ida, is a writer.
Teddy: *Yeah, a hot-check artist!*

I had started the act by saying, "Teddy, let's get into the act," so, after each show, Uncle Manuel would give me notes. His advice this time was, "Don't start out with 'let's get into the act;' you're already in the act!"

Sometime later, as my uncle and I drove to a show in his truck, I remember a dead hamster that escaped from its cage was roasting in the heater vent, and Ray Price was singing "San Antonio Rose" on the radio. Freddy Fender also had a hit record playing on the radio at the time, and he was from San Benito, Texas, just a few miles down the road from Brownsville. Knowing that fact was somehow encouraging to me, and I felt I had a chance at making it, if I just "hung in there." Little did I know that many years later, I would appear with both of those famous Texans.

The summer was coming to an end, so I decided to stay in Houston and enroll in Houston Vocational Technical High School. The first semester of my senior year at a new school in a big city offered many show business opportunities – even at $25 a show, I was already a professional performer in my mind.

I did a political fund raiser for a young politician named George Bush. I didn't know much about him or his party. I didn't even know if I had political views on anything. To me, it was a chance to get on stage. Mr. Bush seemed like a friendly guy and had a son close to my age, but I didn't think either of them had enough personality to get very far in politics. What did I know?

There was an orchestra leader in Houston named Buddy Brock who had a

With Teddy in Houston - 1956

talent agency. I auditioned for him in his office, and I was soon allowed to appear in a few shows whenever the band went on a break. Buddy was never too far away, though. He had warned me about keeping the act clean, and he wanted to make sure I did by listening to my every word. By this time, I had also switched my guitar playing from country music to rock n' roll, and I had put together a band with some of my schoolmates. However, after our band performed a show in the school auditorium, it was obvious that the act with Teddy was my road to success and not my guitar playing! Unfortunately, though, it was clear that girls were attracted to musicians and not ventriloquists.

Before the second semester at my new high school even started, I had already decided I wanted to graduate with my old class back in Brownsville, so I would just have to put show business on hold for a little while. Although I graduated at the bottom of my class, my plans were changed once again when I joined the Navy, along with two of my high school friends, and we all took a train to San Diego, California, for nine weeks of boot camp. I was only seventeen years old.

U.S. Navy
1958 – 1961

Boot camp in San Diego was not all that remarkable. As Recruit Sammy King, I just blended into the company. However, one morning at daily uniform inspection, Company Commander Boatswain's Mate Petty Officer 1st Class C.J. McKinney's boot suddenly struck my tailbone. "King, they say anyone who doesn't shine the back of his shoes doesn't wipe his ass. Do you wipe your ass, King?" But, before I could even answer, I was assigned "head duty," which meant cleaning toilets. If I was in show business, I thought to myself, I wouldn't be working in a toilet. (*However, later in my career, I would, as they say in the business, work a few*

Navy recruit King - 1958

toilets before I hit the "big time.") So, that night, I drew a cartoon of McKinney kicking my ass and posted it on the bulletin board. The "Old Salt" actually liked it, and Sammy the Sailor got out of cleaning toilet duty.

Upon graduation from boot camp, I experienced a minor setback. As a high school graduate, I had been guaranteed a trade school in the Navy. But, instead of going to aviation photographer's school like I thought, I was given orders to report to an amphibious ship, the USS Lawrence County (LST-887), in San Diego, California, 10 miles from Boot Camp. I went home on leave for two weeks, and, when I reported for duty aboard the ship, I had Teddy with me.

Life aboard an amphibious ship was disappointing to me, Fireman Second Class King. Just being a fireman was bad enough, but now I was a second class fireman. About three months after coming on the ship, I read an ad in the *Navy Times* about auditions that were being held at the Coronado Amphibious Base. My shipmates told me I would never get transferred off that tub. They said, "Once you're on an amphibious ship, you stay on it," but, when Teddy and I came back from the audition, all that changed.

I was issued orders to report to Special Services ComPhibPac (Commander Amphibious Force, US Pacific Fleet) headquarters at the Coronado Amphibious Base, where I worked in the office that booked the Navy's band on civic assignments and performed with a choral group called The Chanteymen. Teddy was also a big hit with his introduction to the act, *"In the old Navy, we had wooden ships and iron men, but in our new Navy, we have iron ships and, now, a wooden man."* Happily, I can report that Seaman Sammy King and his "side-swabby" won first place in the All Navy Talent Contest, and we were presented with a trophy by the Admiral. About a month later, I was asked to do my act at a private party, given by that same Admiral, in the famous Del Coronado Hotel across the bay from San Diego.

On board the U.S.S. Lawrence County (LST 887) San Diego

I began celebrating my success a little too early. As I was drinking a six-pack of beer, I lost track of time and soon realized I was late for the show. I rushed into the hotel, asked a bellman where the party was being held, and headed to the ballroom. There was a band playing and a singer on stage, so I assumed I was in the right place. I set up my props off stage and handed the master of ceremonies my written introduction. As the adrenaline kicked in, I sobered up quickly and, upon hearing my name, I went on stage and gave one of my best performances to date. Unfortunately, I had wandered into the wrong ballroom and presented my act for the wrong party. The Admiral was not amused, and I found myself pulling extra "head duty" this time.

The next time I went home on leave, I didn't take Teddy with me. My brother, Morty, was in Junior High School, and he asked me to perform at a school assembly. So, I agreed to do our old Teddy bit the way we had done it in the beginning. However, despite the fact that I was five years older than Morty, he was much taller. But, we did the act anyway, and Morty still couldn't keep from laughing and "talking" at the same time. To my surprise, the audience laughed right along with him, and, the more I ad-libbed, the more Teddy and the audience would laugh. I learned a great lesson that day about ad-libbing during a troubled performance.

I liked my duty assignment in the Navy. I lived in the barracks with the musicians from the Amphibious Base band, and, on liberty, some of us would go across the border to Tijuana, Mexico, and hang out in the nightclubs. The band leader was the legendary Chief Petty Officer, Sid Zerambi, whose almost 50-year tenure in the Navy was exhibited in 12 hash marks on his coat sleeve. Carl Evans was a remarkable saxophone player, and I would work with him years later in *The Mickey Finn Show*. Jerry Scheff was a 19-year-old bass player, a very hip musician, and a great jazz player. He hated rock n' roll, especially Elvis Presley, and I was learning to appreciate good music by hanging out with him. Ironically, years later, I saw Jerry in Las Vegas at the International Hilton playing bass in Elvis' band! Imagine that! Charlie Espinosa was a Mexican-American trumpet player, whose father lived in a small village south of Tijuana called Ejido El Porvenir.

My bandmates and I drove down a couple of times for local fiestas, and, on one trip, I got to sit in with a mariachi band playing songs I had heard on the radio as a kid back in Brownsville. One of the local joints had a Mexican master of ceremonies by the name of Jose Jones (pronounced Ho-nez), whose character I would imitate, saying, "Come on in boys, take a peek, no cover charge. You're going to see Juicy Lucy, Skinny Minnie, Annie with the fanny, and the Honky with the Donkey." I didn't know it at the time, but that master of ceremonies would greatly influence the character and personality of my future dummy; Francisco, the Mexican parrot.

Teddy and I performed at the Enlisted Mens' Club, the Officers' Club, and the Non-Commissioned Officers' Club. Down the road from the base, there was a small community theater doing summer stock productions. It was an opportunity to work on stage again, and, fortunately, the next two plays had parts for me.

As I got near the end of my tour of duty, I was assigned to the

13

USS George Clymer, a troupe transport ship in the Pacific. Again, it was not what I had planned for my career in the Navy. We shipped out of San Diego with stops in Pearl Harbor, Hawaii, and, then, the Philippines, where we boarded several hundred Marines on their way to the Far East. It would take us almost 30 days to get there, so about half-way across the Pacific Ocean, I organized a show using the talent on board. I played the ukulele for four "Old Salts" dancing the hula in grass skirts, hosted the show, backed-up the saxophone player on the song, "Tequila," and performed the act with Teddy, who said, *"Sammy's granddaddy was a sailor. He had 'hash' marks on his sleeves, 'scrambled eggs' on his hat, and 'fruit salad' on his chest. He wasn't a big man in the Navy, just a sloppy eater."*

One night, I was up on deck playing my guitar when a Filipino Naval Officer passed by and stopped to listen. He asked if he could play my guitar, and when I gave it to him, he played a beautiful Spanish ballad called "Romance." I became obsessed with learning the piece and accomplished my goal before we got to Okinawa, where the naval officer got off the ship. I've played that ballad thousands of times since then and taught it to many other guitar players, as well. When we got to Japan, the ship went into dry dock in Yokosuka for the next two months, and I got the chance to see some of the country.

There was a nightclub just outside the Naval shipyard called The Black Rose Cabaret, and it was popular with the servicemen. Teddy and I would go there on weekends and perform for $5.00 a night and drinks. After about a month, the club owner wanted me to start changing my script for every show, but I told him I couldn't do that and still get the same response. However, I tried it for a couple of weeks and, then, realized that without polishing the material, it was just as easy to strictly do gags and get the same laughs.

When our ship left Japan, I was once again just a sailor on board a ship with no outlet for doing shows. I became depressed during the next three months, and I was sent to a hospital in Oakland, California, for evaluation. When I revealed that I was a ventriloquist during group therapy, I got the attention of a young Navy doctor who wanted to get inside the mind of what he considered a "schizophrenic." I started having private sessions with him, during which time he curiously asked questions like, "Do you ever think that you are your dummy?" Well, that was the question that "turned the tide" for me. The doctor would start drooling rather than laughing whenever I answered in either Teddy's voice or the Mexican master of ceremonies character. He wanted "us" to do the act for the other patients, so "we" did a skit in the psychiatric ward, and Teddy played the doctor.

I, Samuel Leon King, Seaman 1st Class, was discharged from the Navy in San Francisco. But, before I left the city, I went down to the area where the nightlife and the shows were located, and, instinctively, I knew I would return there one day as a performer, and it would have profound meaning. Like Tony Bennett at the Fairmont Hotel singing, "I Left My Heart in San Francisco," I, too, felt the need to come back someday. And, as it turned out, I would not only return one day, I would play the Fairmont, opening for Tony Bennett!

With Teddy in a suitcase, I packed my duffle bag and went back to Brownsville for a while. I enrolled at Texas Southmost College and, at night, worked at the Brownsville Police Station as a dispatcher. Being bi-lingual, this provided a good chance for me to use both languages and a microphone. Occasionally, there were opportunities to do a show for the Kiwanis or Lion's Club, but, other than a small nightclub in nearby Port Isabelle, there were no places to perform. There was a fellow who owned a typewriter shop, and he was a singer/dancer who billed himself as "Squeezer Wheezer, the Mexican Greaser." He often took me along with him on gigs, and he, too, would eventually become another influence in developing Francisco, the Mexican parrot's character. Life at the police station was slow on the graveyard shift, and I was bored, so I studied for the police officer's exam and passed. After that, I bought a Colt 38 special revolver and, while waiting to be picked up by a fellow officer to go to the target range, a not-so-funny thing happened.

I was standing in front of a full-length mirror at home practicing a quick draw, cowboy style. About the third time I drew my pistol and pointed it at myself in the mirror, the gun went off. The bullet went straight through the wall and into the kitchen. My brother, Morty, was sitting at the kitchen table eating breakfast. When he heard the gunshot, he dropped his fork, and, as he was bending over to pick it up, I walked into the kitchen and saw him. At first, I thought I had killed him, but, luckily, the bullet barely missed his head and lodged itself in the window sill. After that, I dropped out of college, resigned from the police department, moved back to Houston, and worked in Uncle Manuel's All Pet Center until the circus came to town.

"DAMN EVERYTHING BUT THE CIRCUS" – E.E. Cummings

The Shrine Circus' Texas dates were booked in the winter season when traveling circuses were mostly in their winter quarters and performers were available for off-season work. My uncle, Manuel King, was negotiating the sale of a couple of elephants owned by Dolly Jacobs to a Mexican Circus owner, Bobo Fuentes. It was there that I first laid eyes on Judy Jacobs, the elephant owner's daughter. Her father, Terrell Jacobs, was a big name in the circus world as a lion tamer. Actually, "lion tamer" is a misnomer because lions are not actually tamed; only trained.

Judy Jacobs - "The first Mrs. King"

16

Judy was a circus aerialist with a twin brother nicknamed Punch – get it, "Punch and Judy." Those were the show names given to them by Jack Dempsey, the heavyweight boxing champion, because their real names were Carole and Terrell. Well, Judy and I started working together doing some children's shows in Houston, where I performed with Teddy using kid-friendly dialogue, and I also did some magic tricks, for the one and only time in my career.

Within a period of about three months; I had "run away with the circus," fallen in love, married Judy, and lived in a small house trailer. It was a long, cold February spent in the circus' winter quarters of Gainesville, Texas, and, by late March, Judy just "up and left" one day without saying where she was going. When I finally tracked her down at the Shrine Circus in Washington D.C., she was working for producer/agent Al Dobritch, and she had "hooked up" with the circus ringmaster, Paul Kaye. All she had to say to me was, "Go do something with your life." And, after a brief period of recovery, that's just what this broken-hearted 22-year-old ventriloquist set out to do!

It was a three-day bus ride back to Houston from Washington D.C., followed by an even longer period of depression, but, with nothing else to do, I started writing and rewriting jokes, gags, and ideas for a ventriloquist act with the hopes and dreams of finding a way to succeed in show business. By the time I was finished, I had the makings of what I thought was a promising act. I had "borrowed" lines from Jimmy Nelson & Danny O'Day, Paul Winchell & Jerry Mahoney, and Arthur Worsley & Charlie Brown. Arthur's "bottle of beer" routine was a ventriloquial classic, and I now had my own twist on the bit.

In addition to those just mentioned, I recalled all the ventriloquist acts I'd seen on *The Ed Sullivan Show,* including Jay Nemeth & Nicky, Russ Lewis & Brooklyn, Dick Weston, Shari Lewis, and, of course, Señor Wences. By pinching a line, or two, from each of them, I felt I had proven material, and all I had to do was perfect the timing.

Once I was finally settled in Houston, Uncle Manuel gave me a job in his pet shop. It was not much, but when his poodle groomer suddenly quit, I pretended to know something about grooming dogs, and, through trial and error and a few books, I became a dog groomer long enough to buy a used car and forget about being a circus tag-a-long. I was on my way to stardom...

Theater and Strip Joints
"A Hand in the Bird"

The Houston Theatre Center was rehearsing a production of the Broadway musical, *Carnival*. When the producer of the show called my Uncle Manuel's All Pets Center looking for a dog act, my uncle said he thought his nephew (me) might be able to help them. I had been busy grooming dogs with another groomer; a lady who had a kennel with more than 100 dogs, no husband, four children, and her eye on "the pet shop owner's nephew." I was in-between wives at the time, and Teddy was in-between boxes in storage. The lady groomer let me have a couple of her poodles, and I started training them.

After watching my former brother-in-law's circus act all those weeks in Gainesville, Texas, I thought I'd try doing an act consisting of five poodles, all different colors and all adorned in ruffled collars. So, when this theater opportunity suddenly came along, I was back in show business – not with Teddy, but on stage, nonetheless, even if it wasn't as an actor. The job also included a place to stay behind the theater. And, in addition to the dogs, I also trained a small pony ridden in the show by the producer's daughter.

While at the theater, I met Reed Robinson, a pituitary dwarf who stood four feet, two inches tall. Playing the part of "Jaco" in the musical, Reed had the rich voice associated with a radio announcer. He was an English major at the University of Houston and most articulate. It was from Reed that I learned to speak better English, which was quite helpful in developing my "straight man" character. About half-way through the run of *Carnival*, the cast and producer did a promotional appearance on a local TV show called *Midnight with Marietta*. Reed was dressed in his show costume; a short harlequin smock with green tights, and I wore a pink and orange tuxedo with tails and striped trousers.

The five poodles and I all rode with Reed in his big Oldsmobile 99 to the television station for the midnight show, which was broadcast live. The show ended about 1:30am, and, afterward, we headed home on the freeway with a six-pack of beer, a Texas tradition in those days. On the way home, a flat tire slowed us down, but Reed didn't want to stop because he didn't have a spare tire, and he thought he could make it home. It was about 2:00am when the flashing red and blue lights in the rear-view mirror forced us to pull over. Reed decided to get out and meet the police officer at his patrol car in order to keep him from discovering the empty beer cans in our car. But, when he opened the car door, all the poodles ran out, and I quickly followed to try and round up the dogs. The officer was about to report the situation to the supervisor on duty, but the sight of a man in a pink and orange striped tuxedo, five ruffle-collared poodles, and a dwarf in green tights left him speechless. All he could muster on the radio microphone was, "Sarge, you're not going to believe this one."

Often, after the show, some of the cast would go to a nearby "after hours" jazz club to listen to the Bobby Doyle Three. Bobby was a blind keyboard player and his upright bass player was a youngster by the name of Kenny Rogers (yes, THAT Kenny Rogers). Kenny sang backup in Doyle's group until 1965 when the group disbanded, and he eventually formed The First Edition and achieved success as a pop/country singer.

Then, by chance, fate suddenly took a turn at directing my future in show business. During the run of *Carnival*, the male lead, playing a French puppeteer, became ill and unable to perform. The producer asked me if I thought I could learn the part, which included a lot of dialogue, a couple of songs, and two lengthy sketches with four hand puppets. It was

The first Francisco - 1962

my first attempt at working with hand puppets, so Reed stayed up late with me for a couple of nights, prompting me on the script, and, in two days, I was ready. I rehearsed the role with the female lead, a beautiful young singer/dancer, and fell in love immediately after the first kiss. *That love business came quickly for me.* But, as I was saying, it was my first experience with hand puppets, which inspired me to create the original version of Francisco, the Mexican parrot. The leading lady's mother was the wardrobe mistress, and, with her help, I made my new puppet with a combination of ingre-

19

dients. He was a legless, wingless, pink and green bird with large painted button eyes, and a beak made of paper mache (using flour paste and newspaper from a *Billboard* magazine). However, without any written script, it was still going to be some time before Francisco would appear with me on stage performing.

While in college at Texas Southmost University, I had listened to a record album that would change my life. I didn't know it at the time, but that particular album became the basis for the classic act that I eventually developed for myself and my new partner, Francisco. In 1961, a quartet known as The Four Preps had a mild hit with a novelty ballad they recorded live in concert. It was the Mexican folk song, "La Cucaracha." In a translation of the lyrics, the Mexican character narrating was played by Bruce Belam, who wrote the parody. It was a story about two cockroaches in a Mexican cigarette factory, and, from the recording, I created the basis of Francisco's act, though only four minutes long at that point. But, it was becoming obvious to me that Francisco's voice and character were beginning to change right along with my own.

Born Yesterday - New York, 1962

When the show closed, I took a job for the summer at a playhouse in upstate New York. While there, I played small parts in plays like *Born Yesterday* and *Bus Stop*. I also built sets, which almost cost me an eye. While striking a flat, I pulled out a nail with the claw of the hammer, and it flipped into my eye, point first. So, for the next month, I wore a patch and dark glasses on stage until I left the playhouse at the end of the summer and went back to Houston. At that point, I managed to get a gig in a strip joint on South Main Street, and it was there that Francisco first appeared on stage (between strippers). The club featured exotic dancers, Tempest Storm and Helen Gould Beck, who was known for her famous "fan dance" as Sally Rand. Miss Rand was almost 60 years old at the time, but still beautiful. At only five feet, one inch tall, she was considered an icon in the entertainment world – which I thought was quite an accomplishment for a burlesque star born in the Ozark Mountains of Missouri.

20

Meanwhile, Teddy was still just the rather small hand-carved wooden figure my mother had bought in Mexico. But, coincidently, and unbeknownst to me, my uncle had traded a deodorized skunk for a ventriloquist dummy once owned by a carnival side-show proprietor. The dummy turned out to be a Frank Marshall figure and a first-rate professional ventriloquist model, whose movements included upper and lower lips, eyebrows, ears, winkers, and eyes. This new Teddy required a lot of practice to operate smoothly, and I spent all my spare time working on perfecting the process. I finally put my efforts to the test at a nightclub in Galveston on a two-week booking, and it wasn't long before Teddy's moves resembled those of Charlie McCarthy, Jerry Mahoney, and Danny O'Day.

After a few shows, Gene Whalen, the agent who booked the shows at the Shamrock Hilton in Houston, offered me a two-week job at a club in Tucson, Arizona. I felt like it was a step in the right direction – toward Hollywood. I packed up Teddy, Francisco, my guitar, and my wardrobe (the only suit I owned) in a Nash Metropolitan that I bought for $350, and I drove to Tucson. At 45 miles per hour with no air conditioning, the trip took three days and two nights of sleeping in my car at roadside rest areas. I ate a steady diet of bologna or peanut butter sandwiches, and, at 25 cents a gallon for gas, the trip cost me less than $30, including food. I reached Tucson the afternoon of the day I was to open and checked into the nearby "no-tell" motel for $35 a week. To drink, I bought tea bags and soaked them in hot water out of the faucet.

The club was named The Embers, and it featured exotic dancers (strippers) and a comic doing four shows a night in-between dancers. Teddy and I did everything we had ever done before, and we ad-libbed our way through with the help of a comedy book by Robert Orben entitled *1001 One Liners*. Sharing a dressing room with five bare "ladies of the stage" was a trip in itself. After coming off stage wearing nothing but pasties and tiny G-strings, the ladies would cover themselves modestly with robes while making obscene comments about the ogling customers. Back then, there were no poles or fancy lighting for their dance numbers; only a mirror ball and a tiny stage. The music was played (badly) by a trio of old musicians who looked bored as they muddled their way through "Night Train," or some such tune, as the ladies, with names like "Candy Cane," "Sunny Summers," and "Sugar Stacked," did the usual "bump and grind" dance maneuvers.

At the end of the first week, the club owner told me that his book-keeper was on vacation, but he would have a check for me the following week. So, I stayed and worked the next week, surviving on my limited funds and the generosity of a couple of the girls who felt sorry for me. The following week came and went along with the bookkeeper, who never showed up again. I had done four shows a night for two weeks and didn't get paid, so I was really pissed off…and quite hungry. I phoned my mother in California and asked if she could wire me enough money to pay for the motel and buy enough gas to get out of town. Then, I left and drove to Los Angeles in search of show business, which I found in a *Los Angeles Times* ad looking for acts to go on a USO tour overseas to the Far East.

USO Tours
The 1960s

Jack Kalshiem, a Los Angeles theatrical agent, booked and auditioned acts for the USO in Hollywood. When I walked into his office with my props, Jack was on the phone talking to Bob Hope. "Yeah, Bobby-Baby, I'll take care of it. Have a great trip, and give my love to Dolores." I imagined that I was about to become a USO entertainer on tour all over the world like those great performers I had seen on television. I set up my props and auditioned for an audience of two, Mr. Kalshiem and a young actor named Bob Ridgely, whose generous laughter made the act a success. It was the first time I actually auditioned for anyone, and, two weeks later, there was a contract in the mail for a six-month tour of military installations in Alaska and the Far East. However, there was an unexpected glitch to getting a passport – my birth certificate.

The name on my birth certificate read Samuel Leon Faden, my father's family name. But, when I was young, my mother always wrote my name on official papers as Sammy King, her maiden name. All through my school years, I was known as Sammy King – even on my high school diploma. So, based on my birth certificate, my first passport was issued in 1964 as Samuel Leon Faden; however, with all my records under the name Sammy King, and the fact that I was also now known professionally as Sammy King, my best option was to legally change my name and amend my passport, which I did in 1966 between my first two USO tours.

Along with Teddy, Francisco, and my guitar, I began the trip of a lifetime, or, at least, the next few years. But, Alaska was the wrong place to be in the winter because, not only was it cold, it was also dark 20 hours a day. The troupe, called *Holiday Kapers*, consisted of a trio of musicians (piano, bass, and drums); a dancer, Patsy Smith, who was an ex-Rockette from Radio City; a red-headed singer named Meryl Drabin; a comedian,

Don Cummings, who doubled as master of ceremonies; a show manager; and me. The drummer, Warren, traveled with only two congas instead of a regular drum set, so there were no "rim shots." There was also a bass player named Vic King (no relation) and a piano player, June Derry (who, as it turns out, would be in the audience on opening night at the Palm Springs Follies 40 years later).

Looking back, I remember that Francisco's act did not have an ending at that time. I would simply finish with a parody of "La Cucaracha" and, after that little "ditty," I would play a medley of "La Virgen de la Macarena" (the bullfighter's song) and "Malaguena" on the guitar. The songs had nothing to do with comedy or ventriloquism; they were just something I wanted to do because I thought it added a flashy and entertaining touch to the act. Also, somewhere in the middle of that medley, I always played a few bars of "Chopsticks" in a classical guitar-picking style.

I always opened the act with all the old gags and a few new ones here and there. Plus, I did the "bottle of beer" bit with Teddy. But, my strength was really ad-libbing. I had heckler stoppers for every occasion and some very snappy patter. Whenever we finished "La Cucaracha," I would hang Francisco on a hook under a cage cover with a drape over the top. From the audience, it simply looked like a cage. Then, one day, something happened during a show in Nome, Alaska. It was winter, and it was COLD; so, with Francisco in his cage, covered up and placed next to me, I was playing the guitar and a string broke in the middle of "Malaguena" (*somewhere between the Mala and the guena*). It stopped me dead in my tracks for what seemed like a lifetime (about four seconds) before Francisco started squawking from under the cover – *he did his best work undercover*. Anyway, then, Francisco's distant voice could be heard saying, "Now what are you going to do, Gringo?" The bit got some big laughs because it was obvious I was in trouble. And, after all, comedy is tragedy; someone ELSE'S tragedy. But, the idea of Francisco interrupting my guitar solo grew slowly, show after show, until it evolved into one of the funniest parts of the act and became a permanent fixture in all my shows. I found it rather amazing that I could add a couple minutes of dialogue between myself and Francisco just by looking at a covered cage. Even without a running gag, like "Don't Touch my Feet," I had the makings of an original act.

The troupe played Alaska for nine weeks. Since wake-up calls were either at 4:00 or 5:00am, the most often asked question on the tour was, "What time is the pick-up?" A typical day started with a ride in a C-130 or a C-123 cargo plane. They were so noisy inside that no one could hear anything anyone was saying unless it was by screaming within an inch of someone's ear. After setting up, doing the show, and, then, tearing down all the equipment, we would take another flight to a different location for the night show. Occasionally, we would take a bus ride. On one such occasion, the bus broke down, and, without the engine running, there was no heater. We stayed in that bus 10 miles outside of Fairbanks in temperatures of more than 160 degrees below zero for four hours before we were rescued by an Army tank.

By the time we finished those nine weeks in Alaska, Francisco's bit had expanded to 15 minutes and Teddy's bit was now down to about five. I was no longer playing a guitar solo because there was just nothing I could say, or do, that would follow the success I was getting "trying" to play guitar and being constantly interrupted by Francisco talking from inside his covered cage. One line led to another until I could no longer top myself and just had to walk off stage. Knowing when to leave is an important part of taking a final bow, and the act almost always got a standing ovation from grateful American military personnel away from home.

After Alaska came Japan, Korea, Taiwan, Thailand, and, then, Vietnam. That's where everything changed. When we first arrived in Saigon, we checked into the Majestic Hotel downtown. I was amazed at the number of excellent French restaurants near the hotel. (I didn't speak French… yet, but many of the words derived from Latin were the same in Spanish, so I thought it was probably a language I could easily learn.) Going up-country in "Nam" was usually done by way of surface roads. The last USO troupe that had been there ahead of our *Holiday Kapers* came under sniper attack and two of the members were killed. If there were no safe access roads, we took helicopters. Once, after we landed in our chopper, we discovered 10 bullet holes in the belly of the chopper. We had never even heard a sound!

For one show near the North Vietnam border, we were on a flat-bed trailer for a stage, and the Viet Cong were popping mortar shells 200 yards from the audience of Marines sitting on their helmets in the rain. I acquired that "possum grin," like everything was cool, as I stood there in chocolate-streaked skivvies. Teddy would tell stupid stories to the audience about my family, such as, *"You know Sammy's granddaddy died because of liquor and women…couldn't get either one, so he just laid down and died!"* It was corny, but effective and accepted by an audience where no one seemed bothered by the bombs exploding in the not-too-distant jungle.

USO shows in auditoriums, mess halls, or outdoor fields are one thing, but going to the hospitals was quite a different story. There were no microphones, stages, or dressing rooms. It was mostly a one-on-one bedside chat, but getting a chuckle, or a smile, from the wounded in a war zone hospital was the most heart-warming experience. Vietnam and the war took some getting used to, but, when doctors there told me what powerful medicine comedy could be, I looked forward to the visits, especially in the field hospitals.

Hospital shows meant putting in three or four hours instead of the usual 20-minutes in a show. We would have done it for no pay, but the $150 a week came in handy. I will always remember standing by the bedside of a wounded Marine while Francisco spoke to him. The Marine was only 18 years old, and, when he died, he was smiling at us. I walked out of the room, cried, and questioned how I felt about that war.

The tour ended with a few days in Guam and, finally, Pearl Harbor, Hawaii. In Guam, an agent saw the show and asked if I would be interested in coming back to the Far East and working independently. The only catch was that all acts had to have a girl in the show. I quickly answered that my sister, Luci, was a great singer and that she could do a 20-minute routine in front of me. Even before Luci knew what was going on, I was making plans to get photos, wardrobe, and music ready. The brother and sister team would go the Far East to play Guam, The Philippines, Japan, Thailand and Vietnam.

Luci and I were in Los Angeles getting ready for our Far East tour. I went to Disneyland, where I had seen Wally Boag at the *Golden Horseshoe Revue* back in 1958. He was an amazing comedian, and the show was a fast-paced variety program with dancers, (including one Glenda Guilfoyle, who would work with me in the Palm Springs Follies 43 years later), and a live band in the pit. I marveled at the longest laughs I had ever heard anyone get when Wally suddenly readjusted his toupee and did a series of takes without dialogue, letting the audience create their own internal conversations. Watching Wally was a lesson in stage presence that

26

I valued and emulated for years. Working in servicemen's clubs, Luci and I found that audiences were different from those at a USO show and anything but easy. Acceptance came slowly. But, ultimately, success is sweet, so we learned to fake it on stage and take chances. I'd say, "Luci, why do you wear a bra? You've got nothing to put in it." And, she would answer, "You wear shorts, don't you?" We did every piece of music we knew from "Hava Nagila" to "La Bamba." But, while in the Philippines, there came another fork in the road. *Actually, it was more like a chopstick in the road.* I was working at the Alba Supper Club when Luci married the owner's son. The club was actually a front for a secret underground casino with a speakeasy-type double door entrance leading from the restaurant where I performed. I would first do the bit with Teddy, keeping Francisco pre-set in the wings. So, while I was on stage one night, a boy dancer thought it would be hilarious if Francisco was not on his perch when it came time for me to do the act with him, and he took the puppet out of his cage. I exited with Teddy and returned to the stage with Francisco's cage and my guitar. As I reached in to put my hand in place, there was no Francisco to be found. I saved myself by doing the entire act telling the audience that my parrot was simply not in the mood to come out. Surprisingly, the bit worked well, and everyone bought into the idea, but I spent my time on stage drenched in nervous sweat.

By this time, the agent had already split our duo into two different acts, working two different locations, so it was only a matter of time until Teddy, Francisco, my guitar, and I would be doing a solo 45-minute act. It didn't make for a better show, only longer. And, when the gig ended, I was back in Houston putting together my own show for the Continental Hotel Houston; a revue called *Laugh Laugh Laugh*. Breck Wall's very funny show, *Bottoms Up*, had just closed and relocated to Las Vegas for a long run, and I hoped to follow suit. I recruited a couple of cast members from the Houston Theatre Center; little Reed Robinson and singer Roger Dawson. Then, I started auditioning dancers, building props, and writing material for the show, which was a series of sketches, blackouts, singing, and dancing. Ultimately, it was a mixture, a mess, and a mistake. The show's entire run didn't even last as long as the rehearsals. Needless to say, there were more laughs in the title than in the show.

However, that show allowed me to meet and, then, marry one of the show's dancers, Tita Toro. Her name sounded Puerto Rican, but she was Jewish (*what's in a name?*) and beautiful. With a name like hers, I thought she should be a flamenco dancer, so she started taking dance classes, and I started taking guitar lessons to learn flamenco. It didn't matter that I had no sense of rhythm – that was just a minor detail.

I had worked the Continental Hotel Houston's French Quarter Room as an opening act for Larry Grayson, a singer who was also entertainment director for the hotel. After the first two weeks, Larry was leaving Houston and moving to Las Vegas. But, first, he had a date at a club in Shreveport, Louisiana, for two weeks in November and planned to take me with him. That engagement was cut short by history. While I was rehearsing for the gig, John F. Kennedy was assassinated in Dallas, and the club closed for mourning.

So, it was back to the drawing board and another USO tour; this time to Europe and North Africa for five months. The troupe rehearsed in New York City for 10 days beforehand. It was my first return to the Big Apple since my days as an actor doing summer stock upstate in 1963, which was also the first time I heard Andres Segovia playing classical guitar. Hearing him had a profound impact on my desire to continue practicing both ventriloquism along with guitar, and I still divide my time between the two arts.

A European USO tour featured a home base in Frankfort, Germany. From an Air Force base there, we would travel to the many military bases all over Germany. Then, a tour to Spain changed my view of USO touring. First of all, I could speak Spanish, which meant I could get around the cities and towns on my own, and, most importantly, shop for a Spanish handcrafted guitar. With a little information from a guitarist in Madrid, I found my way to the shop of Jose Ramirez, Constructor de Guitarras Finas, for the same make of guitar played by the great maestro Segovia, and I just had to have one. Not really knowing much about the differences, I bought a flamenco guitar with wooden tuning pegs instead of a classical model, and, oh, what a beautiful sound resonated. Subsequent trips to other Spanish towns close to American military bases were suddenly fascinating, educational, and fun.

Our troupe also made a side trip to Morocco, where there were a few bases, and a two-day visit to Gibraltar. Then, back to Germany and my favorite beer gardens, where, late one night, I made a long distance call to Houston, Texas, (which was eight hours earlier than Frankfort), and proposed marriage to Tita Rosemary Toro. She said "yes," and, when the tour in Europe came to a close, I returned to Houston for my (second) wedding in late February, 1966.

Mrs. King and I went on a Northeast USO tour to Newfoundland, Nova Scotia, Iceland, and Greenland for three months, followed by another tour to Alaska and the Far East for six months. I was company manager on that trip and performed two spots in the show; one with Teddy and the other with the now-polished Francisco bit, which closed with a guitar solo. I was also the master of ceremonies, which meant I introduced the other acts and did some stand-up comedy. As manager of the tour, I was responsible for maintaining a liaison between the troupe and the military contacts, and, in addition, I was in charge of the payroll. Unfortunately, that reminds me of the time in Alaska when I put my pants in the laundry with $4,000 worth of traveler's checks in the pocket. Talk about laundering money!

That Alaska and Far East tour was the same route and schedule as the first one I had taken a couple of years before. The only difference was that, this time, I knew what to expect, so there were few surprises; however, instead of a trio, the music was played by just a pianist and a drummer – no bass. So, when we finished our first nine weeks in Alaska, we were off to Japan, where I bought an electric bass guitar and amplifier. After about a week of practice, I joined the duet on a couple of instrumentals prior to the show. I must have been crazy to think I could simply sit in and sound like a true musician, but it didn't seem to make much difference to the audiences when I played "Hang on Sloopy," which only had three bass notes.

In 1964, we returned to Houston for a little break between USO tours, and I had a chance to visit the Astrodome, actually called the eighth wonder of the world at the time. (I suppose it was a wonder because the air conditioning system created a big cloud in the ceiling of the dome.) It was home to the Houston Astros baseball team, but the night I went there was to see a boxing match between Cassius Clay and Sonny Liston on a huge movie screen. However, I arrived just in time to see the fight end without even sitting down. The memory has nothing to do with my act, Francisco, or ventriloquism – only something that stuck in my memory. Located just two short blocks away from the Astrodome were the remains of the first strip joint I ever worked before embarking on the USO tours.

Our next tour was to the Caribbean and Central America. We went to Puerto Rico, the Dominican Republic, Guantanamo Bay in Cuba, and Panama. Tita was not really happy "on the road" touring, and I didn't blame her. With a salary of $150 a week, we were not going to get rich anytime soon. It would end up being my last trip for the USO and the beginning of trying to "make a go" of show business back home in America. For the next couple of years after those USO tours, I tried to settle in

Houston, and, with the help of my Uncle Manuel, I opened a dog grooming shop called The Groom Room. During my year of trying to be a businessman, I also did a few shows in the area. Country singer, Molly Bee, was performing for one night in nearby Galveston, and I was booked as her opening act. While in the dressing room getting ready for the show, a young guitar player who was working with Molly passed by my door and heard me playing my Ramirez flamenco guitar. "That's a great sounding guitar," he said, referring to the instrument and not the instrumentalist. Although he was an unknown person to me at the time, I invited him to play my guitar. That accidental meeting was my introduction to Lenny Breau, one of the greatest and most versatile guitar players EVER. After hearing Lenny play a Spanish piece, I didn't touch my guitar for two months. He was, without a doubt, the most amazing guitar player I had ever heard anywhere. He could play anything. Years later, after I had met and worked with guitarists like Joe Pass, Herb Ellis, and Juan Serrano, I realized the true greatness of this gifted young man whose path had crossed mine. He is now legendary in the guitar world.

Maria Callas, the opera singer, was doing a charity fundraising benefit in Houston, and Francisco and I were booked as her opening act. The master of ceremonies for the evening was Texas Governor John Connelly. He introduced me with such a heavy Texas drawl that, when I got to the microphone, Teddy's opening line suddenly became, *"Howdy... Hah y'all do-in'?"* Once committed, that became Teddy's character, and he stayed in it throughout the act. Thank goodness for my ability to ad-lib! It was the last time that Teddy and Francisco "worked" together for many years.

There was also a talent show contest in Houston hosted by George Jessel, the famous comedian friend of Al Jolson. I auditioned and secured a spot on the two-hour program, along with many singers, dancers, and even a juggler. But, when it was all over, the first prize went to a duo that lip-synched to a popular record, and Francisco and I placed second. The winners were awarded a two-week contract to appear in Las Vegas with Mr. Jessel and second place was $500, which Tita and I badly needed. I was a little disappointed, especially when George Jessel told me that he thought I should have won; however, that was somewhat comforting to hear. And, it turns out that Bill Newkirk, the entertainment director of the Tidelands, a private nightclub on Main Street in Houston, was also at that particular show. And, in 1969, it was Mr. Newkirk who first booked me into the Dunes Hotel in Las Vegas and, then, later with the Playboy club circuit.

Las Vegas
The 1960s

Back in the day, only private clubs in Texas could afford entertainment because they could sell hard liquor. I was booked into a private nightclub in Houston called The Tidelands, and I did everything I knew how to do on stage, plus some things I couldn't do very well. Though successful, the history of that club as an entertainment venue suddenly came to an end; however, to me, it was for a good reason. The Tidelands became another turning point in my career. The club manager, Bill Newkirk, was leaving Houston and relocating to Los Angeles. He had already built quite a stable of entertainers to manage, including actor, Larry Hovis; comedian, Eric Cohen, who created the television sitcom *Welcome Back, Kotter*; and, then, me, Sammy King, obviously the "most versatile and fastest-rising young comic/ventriloquist/guitarist," etc., etc., in the business. Bill secured a six-month contract for me to do a 12-minute act in Las Vegas.

Going to Las Vegas for the first time is a real trip for anyone, but, for an entertainer, it is especially remarkable. At the time, my contract only stated that I would open at the Dunes Hotel in a Fredric Apcar French production called *Vive Les Girls*. I had no idea I was about to go into one of the greatest lounge shows in Las Vegas history! When I arrived at rehearsals the afternoon before opening, I only had music for five pieces, but the band was 12 pieces, and the leader was trumpeter, Bill Chase, a jazz legend. Jerry Antes was the lead singer, Heather Victorson and Joan Palethorpe were dancers, and Judy Bell was one of the acts. I would work with all of them again some 35 years later at the Palm Springs Follies.

I was only doing the usual 12 minutes with Francisco, but there were three shows a night: the first was at 11:00pm, then 1:00am, and the last one started at 2:45 in the morning. The room was always full for *Vive Les Girls* and almost empty for acts that played in-between. So, between shows one night, I went over to the main room to see ventriloquist, Russ Lewis, in the *Casino de Paris* show. Russ was managed by Eddie Cochran and advertised in *Variety* magazine as the world's most technically perfect ventriloquist. I just had to see him in person, and he was great. His technique was flawless; he popped his M's, P's, and B's unlike any other ventriloquist I had ever heard. And, his act with partner, Brooklyn Birch, was outstanding. Russ had just married, so, as soon as I heard the news, I introduced myself by sending him a message of congratulations from the world's second best ventriloquist. Then, I immediately went back to my room and started practicing and rewriting my material. I kept thinking how foolish I must have sounded when I told Uncle Manuel that my act wasn't ever going to get any better. I looked out my window that night and saw a marquee that read "SAMMY." I knew it wasn't for me, but I made a mental note to myself that, one day, I would tell Sammy Davis, Jr., I had imagined it was for me. And, I did just that some 20 years later in his hotel suite at Harrah's Lake Tahoe.

Las Vegas offered much more of a future than I could have possibly imagined. In a lounge down the strip, a trio called The Curtain Calls was performing. The leader and director/producer was Stan Jay, whom I had met at the preview of my first USO tour, and the singer was his wife, the very same Meryl Drabin from the *Holiday Kapers* tour. Show business was certainly a small world.

Circus-Circus was building a hotel and casino on the strip with a family theme. At the time, everyone thought that was a great idea for the three months of summer, but, then what? What, indeed! Interestingly, though, the acts at this new place were being booked by none other than Al Dobritch, the Bulgarian circus producer who had me thrown out of the auditorium at the Shrine Circus in Washington D.C. so many years ago! Sometime later, I heard that Mr. Dobritch, who apparently owed a lot of gambling markers to the "Boys," died when he "fell" from the roof of the Horseshoe Casino parking building. Ironically, his son, Sandy, and granddaughter, Nicole, would eventually have a talent agency in Las Vegas and get some bookings for me, so they were good folks.

There was a party the night *Vive Les Girls* closed at the Dunes Hotel. The last show was full of the traditional closing night show business crowd, and Bill Chase played a pocket cornet I had bought on a USO tour in North Africa, while Ronnie Lewis, the choreographer, was being celebrated. But, I was on my way to Hollywood once again – this time for television appearances; then, to Las Vegas, Reno, and Lake Tahoe where I would be appearing as the opening act for a variety of stars at various Nevada casinos.

My Las Vegas booking gave the act prestige, and I was able to get into the Playboy circuit. In the 1950s and '60s, Playboy magazine expanded its empire by creating clubs in major cities with the famous "Bunnies" as cocktail and food waitresses. They required a membership in the form of a Playboy key at an annual cost of $25. With over 1,000,000 members, the success of the clubs was launched. The Playboy clubs in large cities around the world booked big name comedians and singers. The other smaller clubs usually booked lesser-known singers and comedy acts. I played clubs in Los Angeles, San Francisco, Phoenix, St. Louis, Kansas City, and Miami, but one of the most difficult clubs was in New Orleans. They had two showrooms with stages back to back, separated by the dressing rooms. On weekends, the club booked five shows a night. As the first show was playing in one room, the audience was being seated in the other room. So, I did three shows in one room and two in the other room, going back and forth. On weekdays, there were only three shows a night total, which felt like a break. I incorporated Teddy, Francisco, some stand-up comedy, and a guitar solo to complete the 45-minute set lasting approximately 20 weeks a year.

At age 28, I still had my left canine upper baby tooth. It was simply never pushed out by the adult canine, which grew above it horizontally. Because it was significantly smaller than my other teeth, I could project a considerable amount of air and voice through the opening and into a microphone. When the tooth was finally taken out by a dentist, it was replaced by a temporary bridge, which I kept for the next couple of years. Once, I bit into a chicken drumstick while driving on the Interstate 10 freeway in Los Angeles and threw the chicken bone out the window along with my bridge. When I realized what I had done, I circled around the next exit in a long U-turn and drove back to the spot where I thought it had landed. After a brief search in the dark, I actually found my bridge alongside the freeway, intact, and buried in the chicken bone. Then, while playing the Playboy Club in New Orleans, I somehow accidentally swallowed my bridge in the middle of the act. But, other than sweating profusely for the remainder of my performance, I managed to successfully finish my show without dropping a line. After that, though, I opted for a permanent bridge; however, it took quite a bit of practice to recover my ventriloquial technique with the new dental configuration.

With the Playboy circuit credits in my resume, it became easier to get on television shows, especially those in syndication, which were plentiful. I made multiple appearances on *Art Linkletter's House Party*, *The Donald O'Connor Show*, *The Merv Griffin Show*, *The Mike Douglas Show*, *The Woody Woodbury Show*, and even ex-football player Rosey Grier's, *The Rosey Grier Show*. Being on Rosey's show was extra special to me, as I had been a fan of the "Gentle Giant" when he played for the Pittsburg Steelers and, then, when he guarded Robert F. Kennedy on his presidential campaign and disarmed Kennedy's assassin, Sirhan Sirhan, at the Ambassador Hotel in Los Angeles. All my TV credits led to many casual gigs, one-nighters, and galas. For the first time in my career, I was actually turning down dates because I was unavailable due to previous commitments.

SAMMY KING   STEVE SHELDON C.D.

My manager, Bill Newkirk, was present at my first booking in John Ascuaga's Nugget Casino Resort in Sparks, Nevada, near Reno. At that point, he was getting out of the business and moving from Los Angeles to El Paso to care for his ailing mother. Coincidently, at that particular engagement, there was an act manager from New York named Steve Sheldon, and he would become my representative for a number of years. Steve had a small stable of acts, including singers, Pam Carrie and Johnny Greenwood, along with a strange little old fellow named Werner Hirzel, who was a one-man band. Steve would book me on dates that I found to be a rather special part of my career, like a summer in the famous Catskill Mountains in upstate New York and my first experience with cruise ships on the Italian Sitmar Lines.

Working on cruise ships required a lot of material, and I was never comfortable with stretching Francisco's classic 12-minute act. I could always manage fairly well for 15-20 minutes, but certainly not more than that, proving that more is not necessarily better; in fact, longer always seemed to make the act worse. Traveling the long flights to distant ports to meet up with a cruise ship was never an easy task either. So, I thought that if I could do Teddy's material (that Texas drawl) with an almost weightless soft puppet instead of carrying a Frank Marshall figure, it would lighten my load. I made Rojo, a red fighting cock (rooster), and basically did 20 minutes of material, which was all the ventriloquial patter I had heard, or seen, other vents doing early in my career. Bits where I was trying to say "ventrickolo-wister-twister" and the letters one usually can't say without lip movement, the M's, P's, and B's, ate up a lot of the time with Rojo playing Teddy's character, and I put my own twist on them like my specific version of the "bottle of beer" bit.

34

Sammy: One can't say a "bottle of beer" without lip movement.

Rojo: *Oh, yeah? Well, I can.*

Sammy: You can say a "bottle of beer" without moving your lips?

Rojo: *Yer doggone tootin' I can do it.*

Sammy: All right, then, let's see if you can. Say a "bottle of beer" for this audience without moving your lips.

Rojo: (no movement) *COORS!!!*

    The bit always went over well, or ALMOST always. On one cruise for Sitmar Cruise Lines, an old lady passenger managed to sneak a pet chicken on board the ship and into her cabin, where she kept it in the bathroom. On the day I was to perform, a cabin steward discovered the chicken, which eventually led to the Captain disposing of it, and the word got around quickly among the passengers and crew alike. Being at sea, the Captain ordered the chicken euthanized and put overboard. What made the story even more dramatic was that the pet chicken had only one eye due to an accident as a baby chick, and the little old lady had raised the chick and kept it as a pet for years. She was in tears at the Captain's actions regarding her illegal chicken on board his ship. At dinner's first seating, the buzz was all about "Chicken of the Sea" and "Chicken Pot Pie," etc. And, then, it was showtime starring the hilarious comedy ventriloquist, Sammy King, and his funny fowl.

    I carried Rojo, the Texas Fighting Cock, on stage in a burlap bag tied with a gold cord. When I pulled him out of the sack, for some unknown reason, one of his eyes got caught in the bag and fell off. So, I was on stage with a one-eyed rooster puppet the very night after the chicken story had circulated around the ship. Everyone thought I was making fun of the lady's chicken story, and the entire 20-minute routine received a less than favorable response from the audience. In fact, I got a few boo's during the act and ended up bombing. That incident cost me more than just a few laughs, as the report to the cruise lines' main office kept me from ever working for them again. I guess it was meant to be that way, and I never used 'ole Rojo in another act again.

    Steve Sheldon remained my manager until 1976, when I chose to take a date in Paris rather than audition for *Soap*, the television sitcom casting a ventriloquist for a part in the show. (The part of the ventriloquist went to the deserving and talented Jay Johnson.) I no longer felt I needed a manager, as most of my dates were booked as a result of being seen on stage somewhere, especially in the many production shows in Nevada. An interesting side note about Steve Sheldon is that he and my mother shared the same birthday, and they actually met while standing in line, one behind the other, at the Tropicana Hotel in Las Vegas. At the time, I was booked there for two weeks in *Les Folies Bergere* to fill in for Gus Augsberg's hilarious monkey act. The closing act was the classy master magician, Lance Burton, and, years later, Lance asked me to fill in for juggler, Michael Goudeau, at the Hacienda Hotel for two weeks.

Miami Beach
The 1970s

Fairs and outdoor events were never very comfortable for me. I could never seem to block out all the noise and stay focused on my act. So, two weeks at the Burning Hills Amphitheater in Medora, North Dakota, with a crowd of 2,500 and a western town setting that included horses, cowboys, Indians, guns, and a lot of "yippees" was nothing like the intimate cabarets I was accustomed to playing. The days of outdoor shows in Vietnam were far behind me, but not beneath me, so I agreed to do a few. However, kids running back and forth in front of the stage, the distant barkers selling cotton candy, and folks screaming on the amusement rides at the California State Fair made me yearn for the nightclubs and showrooms best-suited for my act. A huge fundraising event at the Rose Bowl in Pasadena had an audience of more than 20,000 who came to see a couple of rock stars, but not a ventriloquist. By the time I finished a punch line and waited for the laugh to come back from a great distance, I was already into the next line. Such were the outdoor dates; so, fortunately, I was usually able to refuse by being in the right place at the right time.

In 1969, I was playing two weeks at the Nugget in Sparks, Nevada, opening for The McGuire Sisters. I was standing in the wings watching the elephant act on stage, with my usual pre-show jitters, when the entertainment director, Jim Thompson, came up behind me and said, "Guess who is in the audience?" I didn't have the foggiest notion. When he said it was Edgar Bergen, things quickly got very foggy. After the show, Mr. Bergen came backstage and offered some advice. "You are a wonderful ventriloquist, but you need to believe in your characters more than you do." I didn't like hearing that critique. It was years before I understood what Mr. Bergen meant and admitted he was right. Lip, throat, and head movement control, while a good technique to have, are hardly the most important aspect of performing ventriloquism as an act on stage. Commitment to character is, by far, a finer point of the art. Once applied, that little piece of advice from my encounter with the great master (30 years after I first heard him on *The Edgar Bergen and Charlie McCarthy Show* as a child in Brownsville, Texas) made my act with Francisco much funnier.

After another two-week return engagement at the Nugget opening for Marty Robbins, I was booked for an eight-month season at the Carillon Hotel in Miami Beach. The show was called *Shazam*, a production show starring magician John Daniels. The show had stage sets, magic illusions, dancers who danced, and showgirls who were bare-breasted and wore huge harnessed costumes. One of the other acts was a comedy dance duo from Spain named Elsa and Waldo. It was the longest run of my career in one room, thus far, and it would also contain two very meaningful events in my life. The first was meeting Juan Serrano, the great flamenco guitarist, who lived in Miami. I had seen him on television many times and knew he was a world-class concert artist. Waldo was a personal friend of Juan Serrano's manager, and he arranged for the two of us to meet. As a result, I was able to take weekly flamenco guitar lessons from Juan. I practiced three to four hours every day for the next five years to develop the proper technique.

The second meaningful event experienced during the run of *Shazam* was a big turning point in my career, and it occurred during the fifth month of the show. To my surprise, I received a telegram from Ed Sullivan's show agent, Mark Leddy, offering me a spot on the show. Not wanting to pass up the opportunity, I requested a leave of absence from the Miami Beach show for a week. The request was granted, provided I found a replacement act to substitute for me. I thought of a young ventriloquist named Jay Johnson, whose act I had seen at AstroWorld Amusement Park in Houston, Texas. Jay agreed to cover for me and came to Miami Beach while I drove to New York to do *The Ed Sullivan Show*. Years later, I reveled in Jay's success on the popular television show, *Soap*. I know him now as a ventriloquist giant and a real gentleman.

Going to New York was surreal because I remembered dreaming about it when I was 12 years old. Everything about the Ed Sullivan Theater was just as in my dream. When I got to my dressing room, it was on the third floor with my name on the door, just as I had envisioned all those years before. Upon entering, I got that same spooky déjà vu feeling, knowing I had dreamed the moment as a child. As I stood in the wings watching singer, Jack Jones, on stage and knowing I was on next, Mr. Sullivan came up behind me and said, "I thought you were great when I saw you in Las Vegas." It spooked me and my knees were shaking as I hit the mark on stage. Other acts on the show that night included lone Beatle, Paul McCartney, singing "Maybe I'm Amazed," Norm Crosby, Jan Pierce, Jack Carter, and the Kiev Ballet Company of Russia.

I heard Ed Sullivan making my introduction, "…and, now, for the youngsters in our audience, ventriloquist Sammy King." My act for the show was only about four minutes long, and, unlike the stage version, it began with me playing a solo on flamenco guitar for about half a minute. Then, Francisco would start interrupting me from inside his covered cage. I would stop, apologize to the audience, and bring out the pesky bird. I didn't sing "La Cucaracha" because of the limited time, and Francisco said he was Cuban instead of Mexican, which got a big laugh because it was during the era of the hijackings to Cuba often in the news. To this day, I can't watch the tape of that show or any other television appearance I ever made. For months afterwards, strangers would come up to me and ask, "Didn't I see you on *The Ed Sullivan Show*?" After that, I was never comfortable with losing my privacy or knowing quite how to react toward perfect strangers that recognized me.

Still, the strangest part of that whole Ed Sullivan experience was how everything about the theater, including that third floor dressing room, was just as I had dreamed it when I was young. I couldn't quite get over the feeling of having experienced that exact situation before. It was a vivid picture in my mind that I attributed to either being tired at the time or drugs in my system. I had driven there with my step-brother, Stacy, and my friend, Lennie Savitz, a stage technician at the Carillon Hotel in Miami. We had taken some mescaline on the way, and the effect of the drug was still lingering when I reached the Ed Sullivan Theater on Broadway.

Lennie was originally from New York and one of the positive forces in my career. He was also a humorist and a hippie, before we even knew the definition of the word. What I valued most was what I learned from Lennie about not doing, or saying, anything negative on stage. He encouraged me to do all that I could with my work, saying, "it was all there for me if I wanted it." I wasn't sure if I wanted it, or not, but I knew I was destined for it…whatever "it" meant. I was Sam, the Man with a Plan (an ever-changing plan), so I learned to make plans A, B, C, and still be open to plan "today," which could change everything with a phone call, a letter, a telegram, or a knock on the door.

There was no phone call, letter, telegram, or knock on the door. After about a month, I panicked, and, through my friend, Reed Robinson, in Houston, I met Barbara Jansen and Bo Johnson. They were aspiring actors trying to make it in Hollywood. Bo was a natural humorist and the funniest stage person I had ever met. His every observation came out sounding comical. Barbara had gone to college with Bo in Texas, and she, along with being drop-dead gorgeous, was a singer, a dancer, and a comedic actor – a true triple threat. We had a few meetings together, and, before I knew it, we were talking about forming a musical comedy trio, calling ourselves The Crowd. It was a style of the times with such groups as The Committee. I had two dates booked, one at the Adolphus Hotel in Dallas and the other at a nightclub in Louisiana. To break in the material we wrote and rehearsed, I offered our trio at no extra cost. I thought it was quite contemporary and right in style for the times. However, when no one "jumped" at the idea of booking us, the trio dissolved within three months.

The following winter season, I was asked to return to the Carillon Hotel in a show by singer, Ruey Rhodes, a local favorite in Miami. However, the style of my music didn't really suit the older, mostly Jewish, audiences that were either hotel guests or visitors from nearby hotels and newly-built condominiums. In addition to my act with Francisco, the lower budget show could only afford a magician who was just getting started in the business, and that young man turned out to be Ward Thomas. The

show also had a couple of dancers, but gone were the sets, showgirls, and production numbers, so the show only lasted a few months.

In 1970, Stan Jay, creator of the music trio The Curtain Calls, and I walked into the manager's office at the Carillon Hotel in Miami Beach with the intention of making a show presentation. We had no idea how to accomplish the task, so we decided to wing it with enthusiasm, double-talk, and an on-the-spot medley of nostalgic songs by Stan. We walked out of that office with a deal for the next season! It would be a modern vaudeville show named *Curtain Calls 71*. At the time, Tita Toro (the second Mrs. King) and Rojelio Rodriguez were doing a flamenco dance number in Houston, Texas, accompanied by me, the now famous "guitarist/ventrilo/comic/producer" Sammy King.

When *Curtain Calls 71* opened, the duo and I brought the act to Miami Beach where Tita and Rojelio worked downstage close to the audience. With my out-of-time-out-of-tune guitar playing, and Rojelio's sweat flying out into the audience with every snap of his head, the number didn't have a "snowball's chance" of succeeding, especially in Miami, where there were authentic flamenco dancers from Spain working in a few cabarets. Tita was getting disillusioned with show business, and I couldn't blame her. She and Rojelio went back to Houston, but continued with flamenco dancing for a while. (They would eventually find their way to Las Vegas in Charo's show at the Sahara Hotel.) As for me, I was left feeling my marriage deteriorating. Although I loved our baby daughter, Alicia, my first love was the stage, but Tita wanted security, and that was something very "iffy" for a ventriloquist. Curiously, at age three, Alicia performed my act with Francisco word for word with a rubber duck decorated in green feathers. Kids...

Rojelio Rodriguez flamenco dance company
pictured here with Jose' Greco

By the time *Curtain Calls 71* closed, I was off to New York with Barbara Lauren, a singer from the show, and soon to be the third Mrs. Sammy King. The Catskills had been a haven for entertainers at one time, especially comedy acts, and I had wanted to work in the Catskill Mountains ever since watching all the comedians who regularly appeared on *The Ed Sullivan Show*. I thought it would be a great place for my act, but, mostly, I wanted to be a part of that show business history. All the hotels were filled with summer vacationers and featured nightly shows for the

Curtain Calls '71 - Carillon Hotel Miami Beach

tourists. It was a lucrative field, but the travel from one hotel to another was excessive; at times the first show would be located as much as 100 miles from the second, so that required two rehearsals and/or faking the music cues and trusting the band to play it right the first time. My music was not that important, but the cues were, and I was never comfortable with the very critical vacationing audiences. They could be rude, noisy, and challenging. And, then, there was the time factor. Each show had to be at least 35-45 minutes long, and, at times, I struggled. On one occasion, I came off stage after 30 minutes and the entertainment director said, "If you want your check, you'd better get back out there and do five more minutes." So, I went back out on stage and repeated the first 15 minutes of my act (with the same response) and got the check. But, I no longer cared to work in the Catskills or the Pocanos, and, except for Atlantic City, I never played the Northeast again.

Barbara and I thought that cruise ships might be interesting, and, for a few weeks, we cruised on a popular line. But, back then, an act would get on board in Los Angeles, then cruise to Peru and back in three weeks. With the same audience on board for the entire trip, I had to change the material in my act for each of the three shows. The act was hardly as effective by the third appearance, having done my "A" material already. For me, the worse part about cruise ships was that one or two shows a week would not keep the act as polished as doing revues, which played 12 or 14 shows per week. So, after the cruise, we stayed in Los Angeles, rented a house, and my two teenage stepbrothers moved in with us.

My ambition in life has always been the next show. If I knew I had that next gig, I was content. The club scene in Los Angeles was the only venue for an act like mine in Southern California. Club dates are casuals, galas, and one-nighters for social clubs or company parties. They were plentiful, but never in the kind of atmosphere offered by a theater or nightclub. There was rarely a proper stage or good lighting, but the trade-off was that the audiences all related to each other, which made them more receptive.

I wanted to start expanding my musical possibilities, but that meant a different kind of seasoning. I would have to play music on stage, which was something I knew very little about and had almost no experience doing. I was technically not a musician, so, without Francisco's act, it was a struggle finding work on an amateur level.

My stepbrothers were also interested in music, and we formed a band. Oleander is a poisonous flower that grows in the south and just about everywhere else. It was the name my stepbrothers picked for our newly-created band. We fell just short of being the worst garage band in the world. The music was somewhere between country, rock, folk, and pop. At one point, we were approached by an Egyptian man who wanted to create a "new" kind of music. He called it "Freaky Flamenco," and it consisted of rock combined with Spanish guitar instrumental background music to a voice-over with dialogue that he recited. Some of the lyrics were: "The Egyptians say that if you sit in the corner of a room and contemplate your navel, you will freak out." We actually made the recording, and, then, the man disappeared.

Sammy's gypsy phase

By this time, I had grown a full beard and was wearing my hair long in an attempt to keep up with the times. The band didn't work anywhere, but we did practice all the time. Every now and then, Francisco and I would do a date like the annual two weeks back at the Nugget in Las Vegas when I opened for Ray Price, whose song, "San Antonio Rose," I had heard so many times on the radio years before. (Looking back, I remember Ray asking me if I would be interested in playing Branson with him. At the time, I replied, "What's a Branson?") Things were different by then, though. I was in my gypsy phase and living in a Volkswagen van parked under the freeway next to the hotel; I kind of liked the freedom. I was also trying out my new red rooster puppet named Rojo, who was playing Teddy's character. But, being a bird figure, he seemed to take away from Francisco's act. (The only other bird puppet in my repertoire was an Australian cockatoo named Henrietta, and I used a falsetto voice for her, but I never had a finish, or "blow-off," to the bit.)

The elephant act at the Nugget had changed, too. Bertha was still performing, but the baby, Tina, had been replaced by another little elephant named Angel. And, the girl who performed in the act was also a replacement; the one who had just left after a brief stay was Judy Jacobs, my first ex-wife. She got a job at Disneyland as Tinker Bell "flying" on a cable from the top of the Matterhorn Mountain to the castle at Fantasyland, signaling the start of the nightly fireworks and Disney parade.

The Nugget date supported our band, Oleander, for a couple of months, and, during that time, I thought it might be a good idea to travel to Texas for some musical inspiration. My brothers, Randy and Stacy, Barbara, and I set out across the country from Los Angeles to Houston in three Volkswagen buses. Traveling together would inspire us to write songs like "Ode To Zzyzx Road" (sure to be a big hit), "The Frank Munden Express" (an instrumental), and "Rootin' Tootin' Rudy."

Oleander, the country/folk/rock/pop band

The first stop was in Flagstaff, Arizona, where we set up in a bar to work for drinks and tips. The crowd was mostly college students and the reaction to the first number went from silence to a rumble of disapproval and jeers. Stacy couldn't look up from his guitar, and we were, at the very least, humbled when the subtle snickers and boos became our reward instead of tips or applause. For a while, musician Roger Dawson's golden voice was a part of Oleander, but, by then, it was too late to try and find work for our combination country/folk/rock/pop group, so my guitar playing days were over for the time, and I was once again back to being an opening act, this time with Sonny and Cher at Harrah's Lake Tahoe.

Sonny and Cher were not getting along, and I had nicknamed them Sunny and Shady. When I met them in the dressing room on opening night, they were not talking to each other...or to me. (As a side note, Sonny Bono's new career would be in politics as mayor of Palm Springs, California, and, years later, he opposed the opening of the Palm Springs Follies at the historic Plaza Theatre.) I didn't have any further contact with the pair, and, when the date was over, I went back to Las Vegas to open a new revue at the Flamingo; Matt Gregory's *Fancy That*. After a successful run at the Flamingo, *Fancy That* was booked into the lounge at Harrah's in Reno for another long run.

Long-running shows traditionally closed with pranks galore between cast members. Some of them were funny, but only to other cast members and, perhaps, show people in the audience who came just to see such goings-on. Dancers would blacken a front tooth and smile at each other during serious lyrical numbers, but musicians who were tired of playing the same music over and over during the course of a year's run were usually the best at pulling off musical pranks. For this reason, I held on to my guitar during closing night shows to guard against the possible mistuning of strings. One time, though, I thought I had placed it in a secure location – a dark corner in the wings at Harrah's in Reno. BIG MISTAKE! It was the closing night of a long 10-month run of the show. As the production number just before my act came to an end, a boy dancer named Larry Kern, running off stage and into the wings, made an accidental "Spanish two-step" right on my treasured and expensive Jose Ramirez flamenco guitar. About 30 years later, I would meet that dancer again in the Fabulous Palm Springs Follies.

At this same time, my third wife, Barbara Lauren, wanted to return to her roots as a Broadway musical performer and auditioned for a touring company of *Godspell*. So, by 1973, I was torn between performing away from Barbara or touring with her and not working. I agreed to join her on the *Godspell* tour, and, in Pittsburgh, I slipped on a snow-covered hill while walking my dog. I had a fractured ankle that would keep me in a cast and off the stage for six weeks. As much as I tried to stay positive, I became depressed, so I made a new Francisco puppet, version #20, and made myself available to the Nugget in Sparks, Nevada, once again. It was my 15th two-week engagement there, and I was opening for Ginger Rogers, the now aging movie star of yesteryear (without Fred Astaire), and her troupe of much younger dancers.

Barry Ashton and Wolf Kochmann were producers of various shows in Las Vegas, Miami, London, and a few other cities. Barry was an ex-dancer turned producer at the Silver Slipper Casino in Las Vegas for an early revue featuring ventriloquist, Dick Weston, with his two characters, Clarence and Aunt Martha. The Americana Hotel in Miami Beach was also one of their long-standing showrooms, providing an eight-month contract each season. Francisco's ability to peak an audience within 15 minutes was a valuable asset to these production shows that required time to work in front of a curtain long enough to make a set change before the next number, so I was booked for *Femme de Paris*. The other variety acts appearing with me were juggler, Michael Chirrick, whose mother and uncle, Lottie and Francis Brunn, were considered two of the best jugglers in the business. Also appearing was Gene Detroy and the famous Marquee Chimps, with whom I shared a dressing room. (Gene was an alcoholic and would often take out his anger on the chimps. It was brutal.) Although Barbara and I were now divorced, we were still together, so she took a job in a new musical playing in nearby Fort Lauderdale, Florida.

Ever the incurable romantic, I already had my eye on a beautiful young dancer in the Americana's show. Leigh Cassidy stuck out in the dance line because she was petite and a half beat ahead of everyone else in the line. Actually, I think she was just sharper and quicker to land on the beat than all the other dancers. I was, once again, hit by the "lightning bolt of love," and, before the show came to a close, we were living together. Leigh soon became Mrs. Sammy King, my fourth and final wife.

The next revue would take both of us to Reno in 1975 where I would be in another Fredric Apcar production show at Harrah's, and, next door at Harold's Club, Leigh would dance in a show called *Pin Ups*. The cast included Leigh's sister, Jan, and the adagio team of Spin & Ludo. The show was also backed up by a live rock band called Logic, led by Michael Sherwood, the son of Phyllis and Bobby Sherwood, the famous band leader. I was now into my 20th Francisco figure and Teddy was in storage. I rather liked the idea of being a production show act. It required only 15 minutes or less, and I started making the most of that time by refining the material. I reduced my act to a very tight 12 minutes, and it would remain so for many years.

In 1976, the act was booked into Harrah's Reno opening two weeks for Tony Bennett. I had played in the lounge a couple of times before in production revues, but this was going to be my first time in the Sammy Davis, Jr., Room, a main showroom with a big band and one of the world's greatest entertainers. I thought I could revive the "Old Mac-Donald" bit by having little Reed Robinson doing the Teddy bit. Reed was rather large for a pituitary dwarf, so I had a special seating box made that would sink his butt down a few inches, giving him the appearance of being much smaller.

I covered Reed's face with a plastic clown mask and made a movable mouth by cutting out the lips and chin and attaching a throttle control around his neck to the middle of his back. At the end of the song, I would take a bow and signal Reed to take a bow, which he did by jumping off the box and, then, running off stage. The bit worked well, but I was always rather nervous that he would somehow expose the trick with a body movement. All went well the first week, so, being a rather down-to-earth person, Tony Bennett invited us into his dressing room before the shows for a little casual "chit-chat." During the second week of the run, Reed was playing Keno between shows and won $90 on a ticket at the bar. So, he bought drinks for everyone at the bar and had a couple too many for himself. Little Mr. Robinson was, in fact, an alcoholic and, after a certain amount of drinking, would blackout and not remember anything he was doing thereafter. When he showed up late to the dressing room for the second show, I could see that he was intoxicated and decided it was best not to do the bit. But, Reed insisted that he could "handle it," and I made the mistake of letting him.

I was at the end of the act when I put Francisco away in his cage and started to play the guitar. On the other side of the main curtain behind me, I could hear Reed and the stage technician getting in place for the bit. No one else heard anything, but, to me, Reed's drunken giggling was loud and clear, and I could not focus much on the act I had already done a few thousand times. Somehow, I managed to get through it, walked off stage, and returned for my encore with "Teddy." I announced to the audience that when I first started out in show business, I didn't have Francisco; just an ordinary ventriloquist dummy named Teddy. I said "…and, he's here tonight folks, so I'm going to do my very first act for you. Teddy, come on out here." Then, the main curtain would open slightly, and I would roll out the box on which Reed was sitting, already giggling under the mask. All seemed to be going well with the "Old MacDonald" song, and we got to the giraffe part and, then, the final chord from the orchestra at the E-I-E-I-OOOO. I took a bow and signaled for Teddy to take his bow. Reed jumped off the box, and, as he landed on his feet, his pants came down around his ankles causing him to fall flat on his face. I picked him up and dragged him off stage with a sick feeling in my stomach as a very confused audience suddenly stopped clapping.

Leigh and I were both contracted to return to the Americana (now called the Sheraton Bal Harbor) in Miami Beach with another Ashton/Kochmann show for the next season, and I wanted to put the latest version of Teddy back in the act. This time, he was a tiny (three feet, six inches) Mexican clown named Eliazar, who had been working in the Carson & Barnes Circus, a tent show boasting a large number of elephants. When the circus closed down for the winter, Eliazar came to Miami to play as the third Teddy doing the "Old McDonald" routine. He basically did a good job of being a ventriloquist's dummy, but sometimes he had a nervous twitch, which looked suspicious, and I was always in fear that he would expose the bit.

The Mickey Finn Show

As it turned out, I would be a part of the Mickey Finn family twice at the Nugget in Sparks, Nevada, and, again, for a three-month run at the Holiday Casino in Las Vegas for a high-energy show. In addition to my act, I also played a keystone cop in the opening number, disguised in a costume with a big handlebar mustache and chasing dancers around the stage in a flickering strobe light. Then, I played another long engagement with Fred and Mickey Finn in Hawaii on board Don Ho's floating barge restaurant. It was certainly odd to have a Mexican parrot in a speak-easy-type ragtime show, but Francisco's act was funny everywhere and to all types of audiences. The last time I did *The Mickey Finn Show* was at a retirement community called The Villages in Orlando, Florida.

There are certain events in history that I vividly remember for one reason or another. The assassinations of JFK and RFK, Martin Luther King, Jr., and 9/11 were certainly notable in my memory. It was August

16, 1977 when Elvis Presley died from an overdose of self-medicated prescription drugs. I remember it well because the doctor who made the announcement was named Francisco, and there was an eerie feeling in the showroom that evening as I introduced my partner in the act – Francisco.

Sammy King

Paris, France
The 1980s

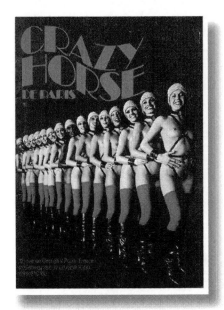

Some of the Crazy Horse nude dancers

The Crazy Horse Saloon in Paris was one of the great cabarets of the world, known for booking some of the world's best variety acts. I didn't know it at the time, but I would soon join the ranks of all those remarkable novelty acts, such as the great Spanish ventriloquist, Señor Wences, who played there for over 10 years. Alain Bernardin was the owner/producer of the Crazy Horse, and his vision for creating artistic stage numbers with a classy twist on Burlesque was copied by many throughout Europe and elsewhere, including America. The show included 22 of the most beautiful nude dancers presented in unusual choreography and lighting along with three or four variety acts. When I opened there, the other acts on the bill were the great mime, George Carl; world class magician, Norm Nielsen, with whom I had shared the stage in *It's Magic* at the Shrine Auditorium in Los Angeles 20 years earlier; and Les Blackwits with Nadia and Ivan Kraus (from Czechoslovakia) performing a wonderful black light puppet act to a musical track. During my third year in Paris, I recorded some character voices for their act.

I was originally given a two-week contract to the Crazy Horse, and I decided to translate a few lines of the act into French. I thought it was going to be an easy transition because, aside from language, the act had a lot of visual ideas. Now, there are a couple of moments at the beginning of each act that serve as my barometer to gauge the level of the audience. But, on opening night, those moments came and went without any reaction at all. There was NOTHING – Total Silence. It was like the prairie, so quiet you could hear the sound of wheat bending in the wind, and it stayed that way all throughout the entire 12-minute act as sweat poured down my face. My hair was as wet as my drenched tuxedo when I walked off stage. To me, nothing was more nerve-racking than not getting a laugh on proven gags. Maybe it was Francisco's accent that made the act more difficult for the audience to understand, I thought. All I knew was that I didn't want, or need, that kind of humiliation, and I was prepared to go back home and admit defeat for the first time in my career. I went back to the small hotel where my wife, Leigh, and I were staying, and I told her to start packing because we were going home.

When I returned to the Crazy Horse at 12 Avenue George V for the second show, M. Bernardin had already left for the night, and, as I told the other acts of my predicament, I learned about that first show's audience and, finally, got the laughs – from my fellow performers! Apparently, no one had warned me that a group of Japanese tourists had bought out the room. Obviously, they didn't understand the dialogue or get the gist of the act, or it could have been the difference between Japanese humor and American humor. But, fortunately, the second show went much better, and, the next day, all three shows were very good. The two weeks became two months the following year, and, after that, I was offered four weeks; then, six weeks. Eventually, I would play the Crazy Horse for six to eight months a year for almost 10 years.

After I had secured my two-month contract for the following year in Paris, I flew back to Los Angeles and recorded an HBO special called *Dummies*, on board the Queen Mary in Long Beach. Hosted by Steve Allen, the show featured fellow ventriloquists; Shari Lewis, Dick Weston, Willie Tyler, Valentine Vox, and Clarence Nash (the original voice of Donald Duck). Next, I was booked in a revue at Harrah's Reno called *Heat's On*, another Fredric Apcar classy production. The show featured lead dancer, Heather Victorson, from the 1969 *Vive Les Girls* at the Dunes Hotel in Las Vegas. My brother, Randy, was now the sound tech in the booth, having transitioned from musician to technician. I was happy, and the show was going well when, at one point in the run, I drove my new Mercedes Benz into a parked truck at 3:00am and broke my ribs. I was on codeine for the pain those first few days after the accident, and my ribs were bandaged. During that time, I was taking my usual nap in the dressing room between shows when I had a rude awakening. All I remember was hearing a loud knock on the door followed by, "Sammy, you're ON." This was my nightmare! I had missed my cue, the band was playing my entrance music, and I was asleep. That is every performer's nightmare – not to be ready in time and miss an entrance cue – and, it was happening to me.

The lounge shows at Harrah's Reno usually had a two-year run before changing. So, it was finally time to make some changes and start thinking about some stability in my life. My wife, Leigh, and I bought a house on King's Row in Reno, and, then, on May 21, 1981, my daughter, Kristi Ann, was born. But, only five months later, Kristi's picture was on a passport when the King family packed up and moved to Paris for my newly-extended run at the Crazy Horse.

During the following decade in Paris, my entire act would undergo many revisions. Francisco's looks altered through four different puppets, each better than the last, and I spent about six months experimenting with "blow-off" gimmicks. Francisco's cage, in its 20th version by now, was equipped with a motor that made the cage shake and green feathers would fly out through a blower trap. The idea was to make it seem like Francisco and Suzy Cockroach were going at it for a visual ending. But, the stunt backfired because, instead of getting a laugh and applause, the audience reaction was silence as they tried to figure out what was happening. Obviously, it was an early period in technology.

Back at the Crazy Horse, audiences were always unpredictable. They were "consistently inconsistent" from one day to the next, even from one show to the next on the same day. I was learning just how tough it was to entertain a mixed group of international tourists, business personnel, and various cultures. Each audience had its own personality, depending on which countries they represented. Surprisingly, not a large percentage of French citizens attended the shows unless they were escorting out-of-town guests. But, one night, a convention of meat cutters from Lyon bought out the room for a private party. They were the loudest, drunkest, and rudest audience I had ever experienced. The French had a unique way of booing. It's a combination of whistles and "woo-woo" sounds that, roughly translated, meant, "Hey, I can't understand what the hell you are saying; speak French!" But, thankfully, those shows were rare, and, most of the time, things like that didn't happen.

"Don't touch my feet!" the running gag in the act with Francisco, came about quite by accident. It was during the third show one Saturday night when my hand was resting on Francisco's left foot, which was perched on the stand. Francisco looked down, then back up at me, and said those four words that would become the signature line of the act. It got a laugh, and, the next night, I tried it a couple of times, and, then later, three times. It seemed to get funnier and funnier each time, depending on the attitude. I knew Señor Wences' running gag was, "S'awright? S'awright!" and, in a similar fashion, "Don't touch my feet!" became my international visual gag. Eventually, it led to the "blow-off" line of the act, "Oh, Suzy (Cockroach), touch my feet."

By 1982, my wife, daughter Kristi, and I were living in a more spacious apartment on Avenue Theophile Gautier, and, that summer, my other daughter Alicia, and her schoolmate Tara Terneny, both 12 years old, came to stay with us for three months. I searched and found a French tutor, Madame Tomasini, who also taught English at The Sorbonne (University of Paris). She was an older woman with a curious sense of humor and a strict sense of teaching. Our entire family enrolled in a quick French language course, and the classes with Mme. Tomasini proved very useful. Francisco now spoke a little French in the act, with a Spanish-American accent!

I had bought Norm Nielsen's Mini Cooper, and we would either drive across the city in the Mini or take the Metro, as the biggest problem in Paris during the day was finding parking spaces. The subway system, once learned, was, by far, the most efficient way to get around the city. However, at night, the Metro shut down around midnight, so it was necessary to drive the Mini to the Crazy Horse and find a place to park. If there was no parking available, I would "create" a spot on the sidewalk near the cabaret.

The summer of 1982 also marked a family drive from Paris to London, crossing the channel by ferry from Le Havre to Dover and, then, traveling through Canterbury's historic architecture, world famous buildings, and beautiful countryside. It was my first experience driving on the "wrong" side of the road. The trip was a fun-filled family holiday, which was extra special for me because I had the opportunity to see comedian, Kelly Monteith, at the Ambassadors Theatre. Kelly, originally from St. Louis, Missouri, had become quite famous in England with his own television program and one-man show in the theatre – both were truly brilliant. I had not seen Kelly since our tours on the Playboy club circuit in America, and we had a brief visit backstage. For the girls, the highlight of the trip was seeing the stage production of Andrew Lloyd Webber's *Cats* at the New London Theatre.

By the following year, our family was living like locals, and we started taking in the many cultural attractions of Paris. Big city life was not quite so intimidating, and the belligerent Parisians didn't seem quite as pushy as we originally thought. In fact, we tended to became somewhat that way ourselves, especially when dealing with traffic while driving the narrow streets and avoiding the "crazy" drivers in Europe. The roundabouts that were so fearsome during the first year became easy to maneuver, and I can remember shaking my fist and swearing in French at other drivers from foreign countries. The most interesting aspect for me personally was when I was asked questions in conversations, such as where I was from and what line of work brought me to Paris. The French have a greater respect for artists of all kinds than generally found in the United States. And, being a musician, an actor, or even a ventriloquist was not frowned upon as much as I had experienced at any other time or place.

One night I found myself in Pigalle at the apartment of Ernest (Ernie) Montego in the company of five great jugglers: Deiter Tasso, Michael Chirrick, Picasso, Toly Castor, and, of course, Ernie Montego. I found the experience most interesting, as the very idea seemed like something out of a show business story – to be in the presence of these fellow entertainers in a place where Henri de Toulouse-Lautrec, Pablo Picasso, and Vincent van Gogh also once lived.

From left to right - Dieter Tasso, Sammy King, Picasso, Michael Chirrick, Toly Castor and Ernest Montego

Life in Paris became a cultural routine and living like locals was no longer stressful. But, the more I was "becoming" a Parisian, the more distant and removed I became from being an American and from the shows and my friends in Las Vegas. In fact, I was almost forgotten there. In 1985, *Folies Bergere* at the Tropicana had two award winning acts performing in the show. Lance Burton won the "World Grand Prix of Magic" award, Ronn Lucas won the Vent Haven Museum, Inc. "Ventriloquist of the Year" award, and I was in my sixth year in Paris.

Our family moved out of central Paris to Boulogne-Billancourt and a modern three bedroom apartment on the ground floor. It was a gated community with underground parking and a large yard where the dogs could run. Our living room faced the Seine River, not far from the Pont de Saint-Cloud. Jerry Lewis and his new bride were going to be spending a few months in Paris, and his agent came to check out our home to see if it would suit Mr. Lewis' needs for approximately three months while we went home. Jerry was considered a genius by the French and, while I always felt he drew much of his physical clowning from Harry Ritz of the Ritz Brothers, there was no denying that he developed his own style and took his comedy to another level. I changed my feelings about his work when I met him and performed in his Labor Day Telethon a couple of years later. Francisco even started doing some Jerry Lewis-type double takes in the act. They were exaggerated, to be sure, but still enhanced the laughs when used in the right places.

Around that same time in my 10-year run at the Crazy Horse, a talent coordinator from a television show in Chile asked to meet with me one night after a show. His name was Enrique, and, in addition to being a co-producer, he was a lawyer in Santiago. We met at a cafe across the street from the cabaret. He was obviously a worldly and intelligent man, and, initially, asked me how much Spanish I spoke. After some small talk in Spanish, he asked if I could do part of the script for Francisco's bit in Spanish without hurting the rhythm of the act. My Spanish was fluent enough to do so, but I didn't think many of the word-play gags would translate well enough to be funny. However, the show would pay $10,000 U.S., and I would only be gone a few days, including travel time.

By this time, I was slowly losing interest in doing television shows, but, during my run in Paris, I had been offered a trip to England to do a TV show in Manchester called *The Good Old Days*. It was a vaudeville-type variety show in a large theater, and my act was very well-received, mostly because I was allowed to do eight minutes of my act. So, after Enrique briefed me on the show in South America, my confidence was high, and I felt reassured that I could do the TV show in Santiago, Chile. We came to an agreement, and, with a signed contract, I flew eighteen hours from Paris to Chile the following month. George Carl and Norm Nielson had done the show before me and said it was an easy date. But, George and Norm did not have speaking acts, and this presented a problem for me.

The show was hosted by a man called Don Francisco, a name that meant nothing to me other than the fact that my parrot had the same name. But, Don Francisco was a big star and the Latin version of our Bob Barker, Phil Donahue, and Johnny Carson. Knowing this fact, plus having the freedom to do my act with no time constraints, I was convinced I would be a hit. So, on the flight to South America, I started writing ideas for material. I arrived two days before the gig, and it actually took that much time to get over the jet lag and feel ready to perform. The first day, Enrique picked me up at the hotel, took me sightseeing, and, also, located a guitar for the act since I hadn't brought mine on the trip. The next afternoon, I rehearsed my music ("La Cucaracha") with the orchestra, which, to no one's surprise, went very well and sounded much better than the quartet at the Crazy Horse. Finally, after a light lunch, I found myself waiting in the Green Room, and I noticed the audience was enthusiastic and very responsive. So far, so good.

As I was standing in the wings waiting to go on, I heard Don Francisco introduce me, "Damas y Caballeros, les presentamos directamente desde Paris, el famoso ventriloco Americano, Sammy King." I walked out with my rented guitar and birdcage in hand to the mark on the studio stage, just next to the pre-set stool. I was wearing a white dinner jacket, wrong for television, and the new Francisco puppet I made in Paris was not yet quite ready. One of the eyes was a little off-center, and I kept focusing on it during the first minute of the act. Then, I noticed that nothing was working. No laughs. In fact, there was no reaction from the audience, even when Francisco spoke in Spanish. I threw in an old Spanish word-play gag about Francisco being called 'Luke' because his mother was born in Hot Springs and his father in Cold River. It had gotten a laugh in Mexico because there were two cities named Rio Frio and Aguas Caliente...but not so much as a chuckle in Chile. Now the sweat was pouring down my face, and I was blaming the hot studio lights. When the act was finally over, I slumped back to the dressing room in defeat.

Don Francisco came into the dressing room and asked me if I would like to tape again, in Spanish, with him interviewing Francisco – "Pancho to Pancho." But in doing so, I felt everything would be out-of-sync, and all I could think about was how Don Francisco and his *Sabado Gigante* show could never make it anywhere else in the world. I could not have been more wrong. A few years later, Don Francisco moved his show from Santiago to Miami and become the most watched television show in the world.

I returned to the Crazy Horse and continued working my audiences with varying degrees of success. But, in all the years I was at the Crazy Horse, the only note regarding my act that M. Bernardin ever gave me was, "Sammy, you must take your time. It's like making love; you must take your time." And, he was exactly right. As I learned to control my timing with different tempos, the act got better and better. The hardest thing to do on stage is nothing. Filling every moment with action and/or dialogue is much easier than all those silent pauses. Two seconds of noth-

56

ingness on stage seems like a lifetime, yet that's exactly what made both Jack Benny and Johnny Carson's long, slow takes so successful.

Charles Aznavour, the French singer and songwriter, was often at the Crazy Horse, having been one of the original acts to play the club in its early years. On one occasion, he requested a meeting with me, and I was more than happy to oblige since I was familiar with his songs, including some he did with Frank Sinatra years before. So, the following day, I went to meet him at his home in Paris. M. Aznavour said he wanted to write a song about the duality of a ventriloquist's  personality and was interested in hearing what I had to say. We discussed the subject, both in French and English, until he was satisfied that, in my opinion, there wasn't much more to the art than bifurcating, or playing two characters simultaneously. I never found out if he wrote the song, or not, but someone told me that he had talked about the idea on a French television show.

It was not unusual to find many world celebrities attending the Crazy Horse revue. Gene Kelly came by as did Seiji Ozawa, the great conductor of many orchestras. Mr. Ozawa became music director of the Boston Symphony Orchestra in 1973, maintaining his tenure there for 29 years. After a performance one night, the maestro asked to meet me, and I was honored to hear him compliment me on my act and the amount of technique I had acquired on classical guitar.

All the variety acts at the Crazy Horse were booked by the month. I worked seven days a week, two shows a night and three on weekends, so, every two or three months, I took a month off. During my time off, I would either go on a vacation and tour other European countries or take a gig somewhere else. Working at the Crazy Horse in Paris was a prestigious engagement, and it gave me enough status to be sought after for other cabarets in France, Monaco, Germany, Italy, and Spain.

During one of my breaks, I was booked by a European agent to work in Macao. I didn't even know where Macao was at the time, but the money was great, and I took the job. Well, it turns out that Macao is a Portuguese Island off the coast of Hong Kong. The show was in a 2,000-seat theater, which totally killed the intimate basement atmosphere of the Crazy Horse Saloon. The audiences were all Chinese citizens, who would ferry over from the mainland to gamble, and the show was free to casino customers. I did one show a night and never once got a laugh for two solid months!

On another of my month-long breaks, I was booked in Palma de Mallorca, Spain, at a huge nightclub called Tito's, but it did not turn out as I expected. The show featured a flamenco production number with authentic Spanish dancers and guitarists. The audiences were mostly Spanish tourists and tour groups from other countries, but Francisco's Spanish with my English and guitar playing were not well-received. While the audiences seemed to enjoy the act, they did not react to the material, and there were few, if any, laughs night after night. After a week of disappointing shows, I let the owner know he could let me out of my contract. It was the one and only time I canceled myself out of a date.

There was another significant life occurrence during my time in Paris; the death of my mother. I flew first class (on the only ticket available) to Las Vegas for the funeral, gathering with relatives and friends. It was a defining moment for me because I remember thinking of all the years I disagreed with her about my talent. As a teenager, my mother would take me to hospitals and retirement communities to do shows for the elderly. She always said I had a God-given talent, and I should use it, but I could not quite wrap my mind around the concept; it seemed too great a responsibility. However, after so many years in the business, I finally wrote her a letter from Paris the year before she died, and, from then on, I approached my performances differently. It was a good change for the act; I became creative again and learned to use my left hand in expressive ways that helped the act visually.

About two years before the end of my contract in Paris, I received a note backstage from a show producer, who was visiting from Atlantic City. The message asked if I could meet him across the street at the corner Brasserie after the show. I did so, thinking that maybe it was going to be an offer to work in New Jersey. But, it turned out to be something even more surprising; there was a new show opening at the Sands Hotel in Las Vegas, and, by chance, it was starting the month after my closing in Paris. The name of the show was *Top Secret*, and its logo showed a beautiful lady winking with an index finger up to her lips signifying "Shhh." I told the producer it was doable, provided they would match my Crazy Horse salary, and, also, provide housing. My experience in show business was typically to ask more and negotiate for less. At the Crazy Horse, salaries for dancers and acts were usually increased by 10%, or more, each year. So, in my eighth year, my salary was almost double that of the initial contract for my first year, and the franc to dollar exchange rate had almost doubled in favor of the dollar. There was no balking about my extreme demand, and I should have known right then that something was fishy. I agreed to do the deal, thinking I had nothing to lose, but it didn't exactly turn out that way.

I made a few overseas phone calls to acts in Las Vegas, but no one seemed to know anything about a new show opening at the Sands Hotel or anywhere else in town. I thought that was curious because show business in "Sin City" was a very small community, especially when it came to show news. As time got closer, less and less was known, or mentioned, about the show until large advertising billboards, newspaper ads, and magazine ads started showing the logo about a month before the supposed opening date. But, still, none of the dancers, acts, or musicians in Vegas knew anything about Top Secret. It was, indeed, a top secret; probably the best kept one in the business. I was starting to have my doubts about the show, even though it was confirmed that the show's producer was the entertainment director of the Sands Hotel in Atlantic City and had been given the job in Las Vegas.

I left the Crazy Horse and took a month off. And, when I finally arrived in Las Vegas, I checked into a room at the Sands, where there was a reservation for me, and everything seemed in order. I walked into rehearsals in the showroom one week before opening, and none of the 20 dancers there were from Las Vegas, which I found odd. Then, I recognized the person on stage directing the stage lighting as one of the choreographers from Paris. The costumes were copies, EXACT copies, of the Crazy Horse, and the music was strangely very familiar. It was another rip off – a stolen idea and, obviously, the reason it was kept so "secret." When word got around that none of the dancers were from Las Vegas, the show had set itself up for criticism of the worst kind. I received phone calls and messages from friends and contemporaries asking what I knew about the show, and I told them that I knew very little. The show opened without the benefit of breaking first, either out-of-town or out-of-state; just a cold opening of invited guests. It was a disaster! Nothing went right, and my act with Francisco was the ONLY variety number in the show, but, even so, the entire show tanked.

A less than favorable review appeared the next day in the *Las Vegas Review Journal* entertainment section labeling the so-called top secret show as "flop secret." There was an attempt at repairing the show, but there was much too much needed to make it work. I was embarrassed to be associated with such a disaster and, after less than a week of poor attendance and laughs around town about the bad production, everyone involved was given notice. I felt sorry for the producer, a nice young lady who was given too large a budget and way too much power for a stolen idea, but there was nothing anyone could do to help her.

I returned to Paris and the Crazy Horse, but I was beginning to feel that it was time for me to leave France and go back to living in the United States. I had learned to speak the French language, and I had learned my way around the streets of Paris, but I always felt like a second-class citizen there. I also longed for the many conveniences of home, but, mostly, I wanted to get back to doing the act the way it had originally played – in colloquial American English. In fact, the only part of the act that I wanted to stay the same as I had performed it at the Crazy Horse was the running gag, "Don't Touch my Feet!"

I had the pleasure of meeting a wide range of famous people while in Paris, ranging from Prince Rainier of Monaco to Patti Hearst of San Francisco. But, I was always most impressed with my fellow variety artists, too numerous to name here for fear of forgetting someone. However, international movie stars, recording artists, and even politicians were often guests of M. Alain Bernardin's famous Crazy Horse Saloon. It makes me proud to have been a small part of international cabaret history.

Leigh, our daughter, Kristi, and I left Paris and moved into a beautiful house we bought in Scottsdale, Arizona. No longer wanting to travel as frequently or as far as before, Leigh opened a dance studio in Phoenix called Dancentre, and Kristi was enrolled in a Montessori school. Within a very few years, the studio became a big success, mostly because of Leigh's outgoing personality, her gift of chatter, and the fact that she had been a successful dancer, which earned her the respect of all her students. Also, growing up and attending school in Scottsdale plus having her parents and siblings close-by was a great comfort to Leigh. The studio eventually became a family business, and I returned to "the road;" that long, lonesome road that entertainers often experience. I would finish my last couple of years alone in Paris; however, Paris no longer appealed to me, and I turned down any further years at the Crazy Horse. In 1989, I came back to the States and sought work once again in Las Vegas.

After returning, I had a period of open months, so I thought maybe I could use a little vacation time. But, then, the phone rang and Dick Paul, an old friend and orchestra leader at the Bal Harbor Hotel in Miami Beach, asked "What are you doing these days?" Dick had relocated from Florida to The Showboat Atlantic City as the entertainment director, so I jumped at the chance to work with him in New Jersey.

Playing the Showboat Casino was exciting both because it was a new experience for me, reminiscent of Uncle Manuel's days as a youth performing his lion act at Steel Pier back in the 1930s, and New York City was so conveniently close. My daughter, Alicia, a theater major at Ball State University came to visit, if only long enough to catch a Broadway show. While in New York, I also had the chance to visit with ventriloquist, Stanley Burns, at his home and hear some great stories of vents gone-by.

Those "spur-of-the-moment" changes, encounters, and calls were something I almost grew to expect, having gotten so many in my career. I was always amazed that I had very little downtime throughout my stage life. I was, indeed, blessed with good fortune, or maybe it was just all in the great plan…. In the scheme of things related to my gift, I never really questioned or lost sight of gratitude.

Puerto Rico, Bahamas, the States, Mexico

Puerto Rico

Leonard Miller was a producer of low-budget shows. He obtained contracts to rooms with shows by underbidding. But, to his credit, when it came to variety acts, Lennie did know and respect their value, and he realized what those acts could contribute to his shows. The El San Juan Hotel in Puerto Rico was one of his accounts. He was clever enough to open a show with first-class acts, but, then, he had a tendency to replace them with less expensive ones. And, if acts were working in Fredric Apcar shows or Barry Ashton shows, he would somehow seek them out and hire them to open one of his shows. Such was the case with me and the show, *C'est Magnific*, a Miller-Reich production, when it opened starring the Caribbean songbird, Glenda Grainger (Lennie's wife); a pick-out dog act; the great juggler, Francis Brunn; ventriloquist, Sammy King; and, of course, the George Reich dancers in the production numbers.

During rehearsals the week before opening, I marveled at the dedication of Francis Brunn. He was a slightly-built man with both the

My sketch of the plane

body and performance attitude of a flamenco dancer. His few minutes spent on stage were the result of countless hours over many years, which is why he remains one of history's greatest jugglers. There were perks that initially made the engagement attractive, such as one show a night and a cabana on the beach. It all sounded great, in part, because I had just purchased an airplane: a Grumman American Tiger, N74614. And, rather than put it in a hanger for eight months, I decided to fly my plane to San Juan and keep it at the Isla Grande Airport to do some island hopping in the Caribbean. Leigh and I, our daughter, Kristi, and our two dogs all enjoyed living in that private cabana facing the lovely blue waters located just a few feet away. On my days off, we could fly to St. Thomas, St. Croix, or remote beaches on the western side of Puerto Rico in less than an hour. Even Santo Domingo was only a couple of hours away, so off we'd go, dogs and all.

I wanted to do my Teddy bit in this show, but I had to find another little person to play the part. So, I flew my airplane to Yauco, a town on the south shore of the island to meet with Batata, a black dwarf who owned a small zoo on the other side of the mountains from San Juan. Batata, Spanish for sweet potato, was a clown and an acrobat. He agreed to do the "Old MacDonald had a Farm" bit with the same ending as before, but, being an acrobat, he could tumble his way off stage into the wings, adding another dimension to the finish. However, the more energetic visual exit diminished the applause, as the audiences were somewhat overwhelmed at the shocking discovery. Batata traveled back and forth between Yauco and San Juan on a bus over the mountains to do the show for a couple months until it just became too taxing on his life.

Palmetto bugs look like giant cockroaches. And, the El San Juan Hotel had plenty of them, especially in the dressing rooms, which were located next to the kitchen. It was like a roach hotel. I had used flower paste and newspaper to make the current version of Francisco's beak, and, one night, a few roaches had crawled into the beak and were eating it from the inside. By the time I discovered this situation, I was on stage putting my hand in place inside Francisco's beak. The roaches scrambled out, and one went up my right arm under my coat sleeve. I had to do the whole act with an itchy insect crawling around. Even with the distraction, Francisco never missed a beat, and when we sang "La Cucaracha," it had a special meaning!

Getting around in San Juan by way of the buses was always fun for me. A bus in Puerto Rico is called a "guagua," pronounced "wahwah" like the electric guitar pedal. Called by the same name in Cuba, Chile, and the Canary Islands, I think the name was adapted from the Spanish nickname for a small child because initially the vehicles were much smaller than a normal bus. Traveling by guagua is the best way to get a feel for the Puerto Rican people, and I could, after a few weeks, imitate the Spanish slang well enough to pass for a local. Little by little, I passed some words on to Francisco in the act, and I could tell from the occasional laughs in certain parts of the script that only the locals understood. I had experienced the same result in Miami shows with certain Cuban slang. Francisco's vocabulary was quite versatile in Spanish-speaking countries like Spain, Mexico, Santo Domingo, Peru, Costa Rica, and Panama.

My guitar playing also advanced from listening to local musicians in small bars and on the streets of Old San Juan. There is a special feeling associated with the Latin sound that I remembered hearing in some of the early recordings of Trio Los Panchos in Mexico and South Texas back in the 1950s. The trio had influenced the style of guitar playing I did back then and later recalled when listening to Willie Nelson. There were always

a couple of guitar players on the beach in front of our cabana that made me stop and listen from time to time. And, hearing them finally made me start listening to what I was playing. I wasn't a guitar player; I just played guitar. There is a big difference. Out of respect for gifted musicians, I dropped the notion of ever becoming a guitar player. The music I played would always be something relaxing, pleasurable, and, perhaps, entertaining, but I was not a real player. By the same token, I would never be an ace pilot, a famous painter, a great writer, or any other kind of true artist. I was good at one thing: walking out on stage, reading an audience, and playing two characters in a comedy sketch. So, I gave my full attention to that in which I excelled – ventriloquism. I built another Francisco puppet and reinvented the material in my act, keeping it the same and, yet, different. Every country in which I performed inspired a little something, either in my guitar music or Francisco's act.

As the season was coming to an end in Puerto Rico, the local tax man came around to try and collect. But, I was a Nevada Corporation and not subject to Puerto Rican taxes. The producer was outraged that I refused to pay. Knowing that I probably wouldn't get my last week's salary anyway, I loaded everyone and everything into the Grumman Tiger and flew back to Florida. Lenny Miller swore that "Sammy King would never work for him again" after the way I left Puerto Rico.

Freeport, Bahamas

Sometime later, Lenny Miller proposed a new lower budget show to the Hotel Sheraton Bal Harbor in Miami, and they wanted me in the show, so Lenny was forced to let bygones be bygones. I opened for the season, fall through spring, and, then, I had a surprise that included another change of plans. Our family was to relocate again with the same show to the Grand Lucayan Beach Resort in Freeport, Grand Bahamas, for an eight-month season.

The cast condominium was located on a water inlet with access to the ocean and having a MacGregor sailboat was the best possible way to enjoy the good weather in the Bahamas. My second favorite thing to do in life was spend an afternoon sailing, snorkeling, and fishing. My first, of course, was performing, even though it was only one show a night during the week. A short five-minute drive to the hotel for the show was actually like having the best of everything at hand. Even Miami Beach was only a short flight away, so we'd head out whenever we needed a break from paradise or to shop for things not easily available on the island, like guitar strings or stage makeup. The most difficult item to find was the right color of marabou boas to make, or repair, Francisco's "molting" feathers. I preferred a kelly green because the other various shades tended to look brown, and unappealing, under stage lighting.

Leigh didn't dance in the show when it first opened, but she didn't mind because she could stay at the condo, which also had a swimming pool in addition to beach access. Even our daughter, Kristi, had a friend her age, who was the daughter of one of the other dancers in the show. But, then, not long after we opened, one of the dancers left the show, and Leigh replaced her with the producer's stipulation that she NOT lose any weight. At only 105 pounds, she was one of the smallest dancers in the line and that made the other dancers look even larger. Always a quick study, Leigh learned the entire show in two days and joined the line.

Life in Freeport was not as wonderful as one might expect. For example, getting a telephone line to the condo took two months, and the lifestyle there was much slower than the way we were used to living. There is nothing I know that is slower than a Bahamian snail, and it seemed like everyone moved at that pace, but, once we adapted to the tempo, it was actually less stressful.

Grocery shopping was probably the biggest drawback. On the narrow roads from the condo to the store, we would pass "The Conchman" in his rusty old pickup truck with the tailgate down. His specialty, and a favorite of mine, was a conch salad made with the white meat extracted live from the queen conch shell and marinated with lime juice, onion, tomato, and a hot pepper. He would chop it fresh right in front of us and place it in a baggie. It is a true Bahamian cultural favorite, and I was especially partial to this treat. And, of course, the fish were good, too, especially fresh-caught grouper and lobster or shrimp, or both. But, then again, I wasn't helping Francisco's voice by developing a "conch paunch." By the time the Bahamas show was over, Kristi Ann was of school age, and it was time to head back to our home base in Scottsdale, Arizona.

Back to the States

Arriving back in the States, I learned that Fredric Apcar was putting together another revue for Harrah's Lake Tahoe. It was still in the

planning stages, so I called Gilbert Miller, the agent who at one time represented Russ Lewis, and had him contact Fredric about the closing act spot. Returning to Lake Tahoe meant a first-class revue again; I'd been there before in *Bedazzle*. The Cal-Neva Lodge on the North Shore of Lake Tahoe drew a different crowd than those at the South Shore. The lounge revue was Fredric Apcar's production

The cast of Bedazzle - Lake Tahoe

with top-notch costumes, music, choreography and acts. When I joined the company, it was the best revue I had been in since *Vive Les Girls* at the Dunes and *Bare Touch* at the Stardust in Las Vegas. The cast included French star, Jacqueline Douguet, with 13 diamond studs in her ears; lead singer, Ralph Loveday; Los Pampas Gauchos of Argentina; and the great statue act of David and Goliath.

At one point, I was in Arizona and comedian, David Iannaci, offered me a ride back to Nevada. As we were driving from Phoenix to Las Vegas, we suddenly took a detour and pitched our combined efforts for a new comedy revue to the entertainment director at the Riverside Hotel in Laughlin, Nevada. He agreed to give us a shot at producing a small revue for the summer. I tried to revive the Teddy bit using my six-year-old daughter, Kristi. She was already a dancer and very good in the part. But, Kristi couldn't stay in the show very long, so I created a new vehicle for Teddy. It was a hand puppet of a farmer, consisting of just eyes, a straw hat, and a goatee.

Our show began as a duo much in the style of the comedy teams of the '50s and '60s. Acts like Rowan & Martin were being imitated more than Dean Martin and Jerry Lewis. David Iannaci was a physical comic, and I had years of experience as a "straight man" for Teddy and Francisco. We consulted with a mutual friend, Bobby Wick, who had worked as a team with Ray Brant of Wick & Brant during the Playboy Club circuit days. After writing and rehearsing material and, then, building props, we were ready to open at the Riverside Hotel in Laughlin, Nevada.

The show didn't exactly attract huge audiences that summer, but Laughlin itself was not typically a summer destination. The temperatures can reach up to 120 degrees, and it was unbearable just to go from the trailer park across the street to the hotel. The show eventually expanded to include Vicki Morris, a singer, and my daughter, Alicia, who had graduated from high school and already done a one-woman show in Houston. I was amazed at how versatile my daughter had become, and I wrote some skits for her, including a "Send in the Clowns" bit, which was a song with David Iannaci as a tramp clown. Once the summer ended, my next job destination was Acapulco, Mexico.

Mexico

Acapulco, Mexico, had a community center called El Centro Acapulco that had a nightclub featuring a Vegas-style review with American dancers staged and choreographed by Michael Darrin. The show had a couple of silent acts, a juggler, and a magician from Mexico, but I was the only speaking act. I was concerned about Francisco's character and how it might be received by a mostly upper class Mexican audience. Francisco's Spanish was more the kind that was considered "pocho" (slang), but still authentic, nevertheless, and very funny. "We" got laughs from key Spanish words that I had never used previously in performances anywhere else.

Strangely enough, the live band for the show was a Jamaican quartet, who did not play the typical Jamaican music, but, rather, a good "rock" sound with a great beat for the dancers, who had been cast in Las Vegas and wore costumes designed by Michael Darrin. The line captain was Pat Gill, a former *Vive Les Girls* dancer with whom I had worked in 1968 at the Parisian Room Lounge of the Dunes Hotel.

One night, the wife of the President of Mexico, Lopez Portillo, came to the club and caught the show. She was impressed and asked me if I would do my act for her husband's birthday celebration. I agreed, and, after the show, the President asked to meet me and said in Spanish, "That was very funny, are you from Northern Mexico?" It was a great compliment to the authenticity of Francisco's character.

The entire cast and band from the show stayed in a large three-story villa with a pool and walled privacy where the girls could sunbathe nude during the day, so as not to get those unsightly tan lines, which was very important to dancers, given the style of barely dressed, Vegas-style costumes. My room was on the top floor with a view of the swimming pool below and a large roof patio where I could make props and catch black Mexican iguanas on the surrounding tree tops. There were certainly worse places on the planet to spend that winter than Acapulco.

Country Tonite
The 1990s

When I returned to Las Vegas after a decade in Paris, few people remembered my act. I showcased at the Maxim Hotel for a show called *Playboy's Girls of Rock and Roll*. It featured centerfold girls from *Playboy* magazine and three variety acts scattered throughout the one hour, 15-minute production. I played the show until the end of the contract. Then, along with my friend, comic David Iannaci, we proposed a variety show called *The Wacky World of Comedy* to the hotel owner at a coffee shop meeting. The price was so ridiculously low,

Wacky World of Comedy - Las Vegas

it was simply a win-win proposition, and we were given a chance to produce the show. There were many novelty acts in Vegas looking for work at the time, so the show opened with many Vegas variety artists including: The Leigh Cassidy Dancers, Fielding West, The New Dunhills, Dieter Tasso, Gil Dova, George Carl, Jr., The Mysterious Mr. Astor, Berri Lee, Cindy Anderson, Alicia King, David Iannaci, and, of course, moi, Sammy King. It ran from January through June of 1990.

When The Mysterious Mr. Astor's magic act was no longer possible in the show because of the large props needed for his illusions, I drove him down to The Riverside Resort Hotel & Casino in Laughlin and introduced him to Roy Jernigan, the director of entertainment. Mr. Astor's imposing figure (six foot, five inches tall, totally bald with a long black beard) and his thick Bulgarian accent was seen as a novelty, so Roy thought I should produce him in a summer magic show for the Riverside Theatre.

I created *The Bulgarian Gypsy Festival* starring the Mysterious Mr. Astor and his troupe of Bulgarian folk dancers and singers with the comedy of ventriloquist, Sammy King, and his Mexican parrot, Francisco. It was a rather strange combination, to be sure. The shows were matinees, so, while performing at the Maxim each night, I traveled the 110 miles from Las Vegas to Laughlin five days a week all summer long with desert temperatures as high as 115 degrees.

Francisco #30

I had several tuxedos and flamenco guitars, and I built my 30th version of Francisco in order to avoid transporting props back and forth. It was a grueling summer, and I was burning myself out, yet loving every minute. Life certainly was not dull, but when the summer ended, I was very happy to have the extra time off and only perform two shows a day in Las Vegas.

One of the scariest moments in my career happened at the Maxim. I was in the middle of the act with Francisco; I had put him under his cage cover and, then, sat on the adjacent stool to play the guitar. Out of the corner of my eye, I saw the cage move slightly, though probably less than an inch. But, I thought it was falling, and as I quickly turned to stop it, the neck of my guitar hit the microphone. As I tried to grab the cage, the stool slipped out from under me and, in the next beat, Francisco's cage, the stool, and the microphone stand all landed on the floor along with me. All I could do was get up slowly, put the guitar on the stool just long enough to pick up Francisco's cage and the microphone, put them back in place, and, then, pick up the script where I left off to finish the bit. The audience roared with approval at my survival!

After June, 1990, the showroom was taken over by Jim Barnes, the Poker Room manager and friend of Joe Burt, the hotel owner. Jim converted *The Wacky World* into *Comedy Cabaret*, a show with comedians off the popular comedy club circuit, which had grown in popularity all over America. Every city and town that had a club with a microphone and light bulb could book a show since the acts were mostly stand-up comics and ventriloquists. One of the best was Jeff Dunham, whom I was proud to have inspired early in his career. For the first 10 years, or so, the comedy clubs usually had as many as four acts, and, then, they started dwindling down to three comics, and, finally, two comics and a master of ceremonies, and so forth, until most of the lesser quality acts burned out the smaller rooms. There were literally thousands of comedians springing up like weeds everywhere, and, when the clubs started closing, thousands of comedians just had day jobs. I will say that many of them were actually very witty, if not downright funny, and they had a very good sense of timing considering their performance numbers. The stage wardrobe, however, had changed from tuxedos to suits to casual wear to tee shirts, jeans, and sneakers. There was no makeup, and no one seemed interested in all that "the theater" had to offer anymore.

In 1991, Joe Burt was granted a gaming license and took over the troubled Aladdin Hotel, which had been passed around through different owners, including Wayne Newton, but none were previously given a gaming license. Jim Barnes became the Aladdin's entertainment director and booked music acts in the lounge, headliners in the 5,000-seat theater, and a new production called *Country Tonite*, a country music show with dancers and various acts, in the 1,000-seat showroom.

When *Country Tonite* first opened, the show lasted a good two and a half hours. But, when it was shortened to one hour and twenty minutes, this show became one of the hottest tickets in Las Vegas. It was all a timing thing. Country music was enjoying another peak in popularity, like it seemed to do about every 10 years. I wanted to stay at the Maxim Hotel in *Comedy Cabaret* because it was the perfect comedy room with 200 seats, whereas the Aladdin production was in a main showroom. (I was still remembering the Landmark Hotel fiasco of years ago.) But, I agreed to open the *Country Tonite* show for a month, with the understanding that if I was not happy, I could go back to *Comedy Cabaret* at the Maxim. At the time, I didn't really think a country music revue would make it in Las Vegas. Boy, was I ever wrong! The show ran for five years.

Part of the deal with the Aladdin show included a room for me in the hotel. When I was checking in at the hotel's front desk, the hotel president happened to walk past. CEO, Joe Burt, was quite fond of Francisco. One night after a show, he told me that he thought Francisco's line; "the Mexican key...Si" was very funny. So, as I was filling out the registration form to get my room, Mr. Burt turned to the desk clerk and told him to "take care of me." Well, in Vegas, those four words meant something special. I wanted to stay in the old section closer to the theater, but the clerk said he had a nice room in the main tower. He gave me the key to room 263, just a short walk down the hall from the stage entrance. I opened the hotel room door and discovered that this room was Elvis and Priscilla Presley's honeymoon suite! I walked through the doorway just as I imagined Elvis had done in 1967, when he carried his new wife across the threshold. It was a room "Fit for a King" – a Sammy King. About once a month after that, some Elvis fan would call the hotel and somehow get through to my room only to ask if I was checking out soon, so they could occupy the suite and/or use it to get married.

One of the more memorable events in my career happened during the five-year run of *Country Tonite*. I took a two-week leave of absence to open for Lee Greenwood in Branson, Missouri. At one time, Lee had been the band leader/sax player for Fredric Apcar's *Bare Touch* revue in Vegas.

But, now, Lee had a couple of hit recordings and was a touring star. I thought my act would be perfect to open for his fans in Branson, especially after all that time doing a country music show in Vegas. It never even occurred to me that I was taking a Vegas act to an area considered part of the Bible Belt. I just thought this was an opportunity to take my career in another new direction. I started a project of making miniature Francisco's, about three inches tall, as a marketing product to sell in Branson instead of the usual tee shirts and photos. I made two hundred little birds and boxed them up for the two and a half day drive from Las Vegas to Branson.

After rehearsals, I opened to a packed house, and, although the act was a hit with the audience, the owner of the theater didn't think that Francisco's material was suited for Branson, and he insisted my act be canceled at once. Lee came to my room and personally apologized, saying there was nothing he could do. I was out.

Sammy King canceled – another first for me. And, although I was paid just the same, it was a depressing time. I packed the 200 little boxes of mini Francisco puppets in the back of my pickup truck along with my props, wardrobe, and personal effects, and I started the long drive back to Las Vegas. About four hours out of Branson, I stopped at a rest area to take my first driving break. I sat on the tailgate of the truck and played my guitar for a while, hoping that it would help me forget what had just happened, but I couldn't stay focused enough to play. So, I put my guitar away and walked around for a few minutes before getting back in the truck and driving off. Just when I thought things couldn't get any worse, I was proven wrong again. At the next roadside rest area, I discovered that the tailgate to the truck was still down and the box containing all 200 miniature puppets was gone. My three months of work was somewhere on the highway!

Back at the Aladdin, things were, at least, assuring and comfortable on stage. About the time I was getting over the Branson disaster, there was a different kind of derailment one night during a performance. A bat was in the showroom and picked the middle of my act to start buzzing the room. The bat made a couple of passes over the audience and around Francisco and me on stage, and, then, flew off somewhere backstage. Francisco followed its flight pattern and said, "What was that? If it's a parakeet, I'm going to nail her." But, everyone had seen the bat, and the focus was no longer on the performance. It seemed like a very long time before I could find my place in the act. It was a dramatic pause that went from a couple of seconds to a good minute during which nothing was said on stage. Finally, Francisco started doing pantomime facial expressions to someone in the audience, and I was back in the act. But, that minute of quiet seemed like a lifetime with no one to save me. Being lost on stage is a terribly fearful feeling.

I was in *Country Tonite* for almost a year before I got to know any of the cast very well. Because I lived just down the hall, I was in and out of the show and back to my room before the band even finished the finale and went to their dressing rooms. But, when I finally made the effort, I met Buzz Evans, the steel guitar player. He also played guitar with a great touch, which made it sound a lot like a pedal steel. One night, in conversation, Molly Bee's guitar player Lenny Breau's name came up, and I mentioned that I had met him years earlier in my career. Well, Buzz and I soon became friends, and he would help me learn to be more confident about my guitar playing.

One very special day in my hotel suite at the Aladdin was when local ventriloquist, Joel Leder, brought fellow vent, Dick Weston, over for a social visit. I had admired Dick's act ever since I first saw him on *The Ed Sullivan Show* 35 years earlier. Since then, we had worked together once on the HBO special, *Dummies*, but we didn't really get to visit much at the time. Dick was very thin, not well, and at the end of his days. But, it was so good to sit together and listen to all those show business stories of yesteryear. I remember thinking that someday I, too, would have to face the same reality…if I lived that long.

The producer of *Country Tonite* was pleased to announce that he had gotten a call from *The Tonight Show Starring Johnny Carson* asking for my act. They were going to tape in Las Vegas for a couple of weeks, and the talent coordinator had seen my act at the Aladdin and wanted to book me for the show. But, I declined and said I would rather NOT do the show. I had turned down one of the most popular shows on television and actually felt good about my reasons.

During the five years I lived and worked in *Country Tonite*, there were many changes that would still affect the quality of my act, even after thousands of performances and all those years. One major transformation came in the form of students – I found myself becoming a teacher; a tutor or instructor. I used my extensive experience to create ways of refining other performer's acts. While some of my students were ventriloquists, I didn't teach Ventriloquism 101. My mentoring was more about the finer points of performing and communicating with an audience. I was becoming a coach…yet still very much a performer.

A highlight of my life occurred in 1996 when I performed for Señor Wences' 100th birthday at the Valentine Vox Ventriloquist Museum in Las Vegas. Several other vents were on the show, but Francisco threw in some extra lines in Spanish that got a smile out of one of the world's most famous ventriloquists. I was elated. I had performed in front of Edgar Bergen, Jimmy Nelson, Paul Winchell, Shari Lewis, and, now, Señor Wences. It was all part of my destiny and right in line with all my childhood dreams. There is a lot to be said for dreams and imagination, and I would often stress that to aspiring ventriloquists.

After *Country Tonite*, I worked on another two-week cruise to the Caribbean for Royal Caribbean Cruise Lines, and, upon my return, I got a call from comedy magician Larry Wilson, about a date in Lake Tahoe. It's interesting how most of my engagements just fell into place at the right time. Larry was producing a show for Harvey's Hotel on South Shore called *Super Heroes of Comedy*. The show would feature comedy juggler, Michael Goudeau; ventriloquist, Sammy King; and Larry's subtle and smart comedy magic. There were also four ladies in the show, working as assistants to Larry in helping move his large illusions around the stage.

The show alternated in the theater with jazz singer and guitarist Kenny Rankin, a unique stylist who was quite popular in the 1970s. Rankin's unique gift for reworking classic songs like "Blackbird" by the Beatles impressed Paul McCartney so much that Paul asked Rankin to perform his version when he and John Lennon were inducted into the Songwriters Hall of Fame. At Harvey's Hotel, Rankin and I had dressing rooms next to each other, and, after my act one night, I was in his room sharing my particular version of the Beatles' tune, when I suddenly heard the announcement in the finale, "…and, ventriloquist Sammy King." I scrambled down the stairs to the stage and, on the way, missed a step and jammed a vertebra in my back, pinching a nerve that crippled me for a week. Unable to walk without crutches, I had to enter the stage in a blackout and exit the same way. Once again, I was experiencing the performer's nightmare of missing a cue.

Biloxi and Horse Play

"I'm an old cowhand, from the Rio Grande."

Las Vegas Nights was a Greg Thompson production show at the Grand Hotel in Biloxi, Mississippi. It was the closest thing to a vaudeville show I had ever experienced because instead of the usual two or three acts in most production shows, this one had six acts. As a result of being seen in *Country Tonite* at the Aladdin, my act was booked as a favor to the Grand Hotel's president. In other words, the act booked itself. The cast of *Las Vegas Nights* in Biloxi included John Stoltz's motorcycle globe of death act;

Las Vegas Nights - the Grand Hotel, Biloxi

juggler, Anthony Gatto; Bobby Moore's dog act; the French silk aerialist, Isabelle; magician, James Brandon; two singers; ventriloquist, Sammy King with Francisco; and a line of beautiful dancers. I shared a dressing room with magician, James Brandon. He had a flock of pigeons laying eggs in the dressing room. They tasted pretty good, too….not the pigeons, the eggs. Yes, they were actually pigeons instead of the usual doves most magicians use. The pigeons were somewhat larger than doves, but all white, nevertheless, and just as effective, if not even more so. I liked them because I didn't have to care for them. Their constant cooing, seeds and droppings on the floor, and feathers everywhere were a reminder that Francisco was a low-maintenance bird, and it was definitely an advantage being a ventriloquist. A magician spends a lot of time loading and preparing props for each and every show. A ventriloquist has only to open a case.

One morning, during breakfast in a restaurant, I got the idea of bringing Teddy back into the act by way of a different vehicle – a horse, a miniature horse. I would bill him as "The World's Smallest Singing Horse." It sounded like a good pitch to me. After all, Frances, the talking Army mule, had been very successful in movies with Donald O'Connor. And, having appeared a couple of times on *The Donald O'Connor Show*, it just seemed to follow that I could also be successful with my talking horse. Everything was falling in place just like all the other bizarre moves in my career.

There were a couple of vents around who were doing their acts with live dogs using a false jaw gimmick. For example, in Las Vegas, Andre used a remote control to move the dog's false lower jaw, but the sync was always a little off. It looked like a foreign movie being translated into English. In Branson, Missouri, Todd Oliver was performing a hilarious act on the Branson Belle Showboat using a very clever device in the leash of his three different dogs: Irving, Lucy, and Elvis. Also, Todd's smile was very appealing, and he could encourage laughter from an audience by laughing at his situation. According to Todd, Andre threatened to sue him for stealing his idea, but nothing ever came of that threat. The idea had actually been done years before in Europe. There is something to be said for kids, dogs, and banjos on stage; they are a hard act to follow. I recalled training a Shetland pony at the Houston Theatre Center years before, and I thought a horse might be perfect for the "Old MacDonald" bit, with Teddy dressed as a cowboy.

A month before the show closed, I made several visits to a couple of miniature horse farms in Mississippi. Finally, I found the right horse with the right temperament and size. Although he was still too young to be taken away, I left a deposit on him, and I started planning my "new" act with Teddy. After a few visits to the farm to try and get a feel for the whole idea, I bought a van and converted it to a transportation vehicle for the little horse. His original name was Native Son, but I changed it; first to Pee Wee, then Thunderbolt, and, finally, "Goliath, the World's Smallest Singing Horse." After the necessary preparations, like health certificates and castration, we were ready for the long haul from Biloxi to Las Vegas as soon as the show closed. Now, THERE'S a good idea – cut off a horse's testicles, put him in a mini-van for the first time in his life, and drive a couple thousand miles across America. So very wrong!

The trip in the van started out in a heavy rainstorm, and, in Louisiana, we ended up on the side of the Interstate with a blown engine. We waited there for many hours until Uncle Manuel once again came to my rescue, driving from Houston with a trailer. It would take a long time of traveling, training, rehearsing, and prop building before Teddy rode out on stage as "Buckaroo Buddy on Goliath." I had made a miniature saddle with saddle bags for the horse. His harness had a specially-built control cable that looked like a dangling rope, and the bridle bit had the necessary mouth-moving control. I kept the control in my left hand, and my right hand in Buckaroo Buddy (Teddy). It took two months, with stops in Houston, Phoenix, and Las Vegas before we finally reached Reno.

I opened for the Spanish singer/comedian/guitar player, Charo, at the Nugget in Sparks, Nevada, for a second time, and Goliath made his stage debut to an audience of about 700. To keep his hoofs from slipping on the slick stage, I had the stage technicians roll out a red carpet, and, when we made our entrance, Goliath froze half-way to the microphone. He wouldn't move. Charo loved the little horse and had me bring him to her dressing room, where she spoke in Spanish, apparently to amuse herself and the horse. I had rehearsed walking out on stage with Goliath about ten times with no one in the showroom, and, after a few tries, the cute little guy was just fine with the idea. But, when the audience first saw him walk out on stage, the loud chorus of "awe's" made Goliath a little nervous, and, when we finally got to the microphone, he was ready to

Buckaroo Buddy and Goliath

call it a night. There is no stopping a horse of any size who wants to back up. So, when I started singing "Old MacDonald had a Farm, E I E I O," Goliath slowly backed up all the way off the stage.

After a few more shows, my little horse eventually got the hang of things, and the bit was effective and strong, but it was a different internal conversation for the audience, and it took away from the act, just like Francisco's shaking cage in Paris or the tumbling dwarf in Puerto Rico. Buckaroo Buddy and Goliath worked a couple of private parties in Los Angeles, and, then, we did a show for the Retired Rodeo Cowboys Association at the National Finals Rodeo in Las Vegas at Circus Circus Hotel. It was the last time Teddy performed with Goliath, who was retired to a mini-horse ranch, but not as a stud.

An agent who had seen the show at Circus Circus asked if I would do my act with Francisco at the New York-New York Hotel in a banquet room for managers of a fast-food chain. For some reason, they were mostly Mexican-Americans, and the theme for the event was Latino. Since there wasn't a band for the act, and I didn't want to use a CD for the music, I performed the act with my daughter, Kristi, as the lone Mariachi playing maracas and dressed in a Latin show costume. We had a very positive response as she stood next to Francisco, who called her Bonita Rosita Chiquita and did some ad-lib improvisational material in "Spanglish."

The next time the phone rang, I would receive an offer to go to Mexico City in a show called *Crazy de Paris*, another knock-off of the

Crazy Horse in Paris. Magician, Norm Nielsen, was out of semi-retirement doing his act in the show and needed someone to fill in for a few weeks. The show was an exact copy of the Crazy Horse in Paris including costumes, wigs, music, stage sets, and lighting. Even the girls were French imports, all 12 of them. There were, at least, 10 of these shows around the world by would-be producers stealing the idea.

At first, working in Mexico appealed to me because of the positive reactions Francisco and I always received. What I had forgotten was that Mexico is the land of manana, which is "everything gets done tomorrow, and tomorrow never comes." After three months and three weeks without being paid, I went back to Las Vegas. The show's three producers all took turns calling me from Mexico, asking me to come back and making promises about the money situation. Finally, I got a call from agent, Bernard Hilda, in Paris. He had contracted the dancers in the show and had also booked my act in a couple of European galas. After assuring me I would get my money, I told him I would return to Mexico City and finish my contract. However, the show was not doing well, a problem I attributed to the number of "owners," and it closed the following month. I returned to Las Vegas in time for a phone call from Charo asking me to work in her revue at the Sahara Hotel for a few of months, to which I gladly agreed.

It seemed rather odd to me that Charo would actually think my act was good for her show since Francisco and Charo's character were, in my mind, very similar. There was all the word play, mispronunciations, Spanish accent, and flamenco guitar playing. To a certain extent, I was right, but, then again, the audiences she drew were already primed for that sort of comedy, so I had little trouble getting past the acceptance factor. Charo also wanted me to bring my miniature horse into the show, but the show's producer, John Stewart, was not willing to pay extra for the short bit that would be an additional three minutes.

I finished the show at the Sahara and left Las Vegas for another two-week cruise date on a Princess Cruise Line ship, this time to Alaska. Since the passengers on board were families of all ages, Francisco's act was family-friendly, not much different from the Vegas version, but enough to be "cruise ship appropriate." Even Teddy's script was revised:

Teddy: *You know what the biggest problem with the world is today?*
Sammy: What?
Teddy: *Too many KIDS.*
Sammy: Too many kids???
Teddy: *That's right. There is a woman giving birth to a baby every three minutes.*
Sammy: Every three minutes?
Teddy: *Yeah, we've got to find that woman and STOP her!*

If I popped the "P" in STOP, it always got a laugh. If I didn't, it sounded like "...we've got to find that woman and STAWK her," and I could feel the "huh?" from the audience. I never was that great at the tougher letters of the alphabet, so, if I slipped, I would repeat the sentence in my own voice to save myself.

I had not seen the North Country since my USO days, and summer was a great season for travel to that area. I joined the ship in Vancouver, British Columbia, arriving there a day ahead of time. I took a taxi downtown to visit The Cave, where I had opened for The Mills Brothers, Bobbie Gentry, and Connie Stevens so many years before. Sadly, I found that the club was gone, like most of the sedate supper clubs of yesteryear when men wore suits, ladies dressed "to the nines," and the entertainment included fine dining and dancing cheek-to-cheek. Show business, as I once knew it, was changing and I thought maybe I should be doing the same. I thought it was the story of my life on stage; always evolving. Looking back, I realized that even though I was doing the same act, I was always doing it differently. I had created and performed with more than 30 different Francisco puppets and done Teddy's old act with about 10 different figures and characters.

Enter Riff Markowitz, and my life was about to change once again...

The Fabulous Palm Springs Follies
Season X, 2000-2001

Riff Markowitz, producer and managing director of the Fabulous Palm Springs Follies, had seen my act in *Country Tonite* at the Aladdin Hotel in Las Vegas, and, at the "meet and greet" after the show, he asked my age and handed me his business card. It was the first time anyone had ever asked me that question in a greeting. But, when he explained that no one in the cast of his show in California was younger than 55, I was curious as to what kind of show he was producing. He suggested I check it out at some point, but I was not really interested. However, the next year, while driving from Los Angeles to Las Vegas, I stopped in Palm Springs one afternoon and was totally amazed at what I saw. The show was a first-class production that featured dancers between the ages of 55 and 85, most of them closer to 85. Palm Springs was a very artsy town with a history of being a playground for the famous Hollywood stars of the 1930s and '40s. George Burns had called it "God's waiting room for aging entertainers." Many celebrities had second homes in the area, including Bob Hope, Frank Sinatra, Dean Martin, Lucille Ball and Desi Arnaz, Gene Autry, Dinah Shore, and Elvis Presley. Many of the streets in the area were named after these older stars.

My drawing of the Plaza Theatre, Palm Springs

The Plaza Theatre, in the center of town, was built in 1936 as a movie theater and home to Jack Benny's radio show broadcast. The Palm Springs Follies was already in its tenth year, playing five days a week starting with a matinee on Wednesday and ending with the matinee on Sunday. This schedule gave the cast a three-night "weekend" off each week. It was a great gig for any act, and, happily, I was given an eight-month season's contract. Being a movie theater originally, the audience was seated facing the stage, which was so much easier to play than the configuration of cabarets and showrooms in Las Vegas where tables spread the audiences apart so waitresses could deliver drinks. Also, the sound system was excellent, and there wasn't the general noise of a cabaret.

Opening night of Follies X was as nerve-wracking as any other opening night, but Francisco and I got the best response our act had received since the days of USO tours. As the weeks went by, Francisco became somewhat of a Follies mascot. The ushers took a survey after each performance, rating various aspects of the show, and Francisco's "Don't Touch my Feet!" became a byword. It was the catch phrase everyone repeated on the tour buses. Four, or five, busloads a day were brought to the Follies from retirement communities and in touring groups. Many celebrities also attended, including Paul Winchell, who was now a resident in the Coachella Valley. He and I met in the lobby after a show one night, and the vent mentor invited me to lunch. What a great honor for a ventriloquist! I felt this meeting was a fulfillment of my destiny.

As we enjoyed our lunch together, Dr. Winchell and I shared how much we had in common despite being a generation apart. Of course, I was in awe of the great maestro and, at the same time, felt very relaxed and at ease as we discussed our similarities, such as speaking various languages, hometowns named Brownsville (his in New York, mine in Texas), but, strangely enough, we never talked about ventriloquism. Dr. Winchell was mostly complimentary toward me, but, at one point, he suggested that I change my name to Alejandro, or something similar. "Sammy is a name for a Jewish comedian from Brownsville, but the one in Brooklyn...," he remarked. I thought he was probably right, but, after all my years in the business, a name change just wasn't going to happen. To my delight, Dr. Winchell and I met a second time for lunch, and he showed me his home, his paintings, and the books he had written. He even asked if I would be interested in collaborating with him on a future book, while he was still "young enough to remember."

Show business at the Follies was the most regimented of all my experiences. The rules were strict, and there were no exceptions. Each act was escorted from the dressing room to the stage to avoid any missed cues. At each door along the way, the escort would knock twice and announce "coming in" or "coming out" before opening a door to minimize the possibility of a collision between cast member and crew. The smallest detail, such as not dipping into the popcorn bowl in the green room, was a rule to keep from spreading germs. It was a good idea since almost everyone was older and more susceptible to illnesses, causing necessary cast member rearrangements on stage. An additional perk was having wardrobe picked up at the end of each week and taken to the dry cleaners. After the two-day weekend off, the wardrobe would be found hanging

Sammy King at the "meet and greet" after the Follies show

back in the dressing room. A first-class, fully furnished condominium was also provided for the acts. There were many such advantages to working in one of the classiest productions I had ever had the pleasure of experiencing. The Palm Springs Follies was not unlike Florenz Ziegfeld's Follies on Broadway, except for the age of the cast. There were dressers to help each dancer/singer with quick changes, and, between numbers, a large number of technicians and crew to move the show along smoothly and with precise timing. At the "meet and greet" after each performance, the cast, still in finale costumes, shook hands with the audiences at the exits wearing white gloves to keep from getting germs, and even the gloves were washed after each use.

My first year in Follies X had a cast of 20 singers and dancers and four great novelty acts: The vaudevillian Mercer Brothers, Bud and Jim;

juggler, Nino Frediani; a dog act; and Francisco, the Mexican parrot. In addition to the variety artists, the show also featured such closing act stars as Donald O'Conner, Tony Martin, Howard Keel, Carol Lawrence, Kaye Ballard, the Four Aces, and John Davidson. Because of the age of the cast, each act had a private dressing room with a TV and lounge chair, bathroom, and a "quiet room" for those who wanted to nap between

Ladies and Gentlemen of the Palm Springs Follies

shows on two-show days. No one was allowed back stage, in the green room, or in the dressing rooms without a show pass worn for identification. Riff Markowitz's Follies was, to say the least, a very well-run operation and the best disciplined show, even if somewhat over the top.

About half-way through the season, a business card was delivered to my dressing room shortly after doing my act. The name Frank D. Yturria, Brownsville, Texas, was on the front of the card, and, on the back, there was a handwritten note asking if I was related to Manuel King, and, if so, to please call. The following morning, I called the number on the card and spoke to Mr. Yturria, confirming that I was, indeed, Manuel's nephew. He began a conversation about attending school with my uncle back in Texas, and asked if I would be so kind as to have dinner with him and his wife, Mary. I agreed, we set a date, time, and place, and I met them at a fine restaurant in nearby Rancho Mirage, California. The Yturria family was very well-known in my hometown, and, growing up, I had heard the name. Mr. Yturria was a rather legendary rancher and conservationist, and, as a boy, delighted in visiting Snakeville to see all the animals. He asked if I would perform my act at the Yturria Ranch in South Texas for a "little" party he was giving. I said I would, and, when the Follies closed, I went back to my hometown for the party, which was anything but "little!" Mr. Yturria's guest list included some very famous politicians and socialites among the 200 guests attending a western-style barbeque in a huge air-conditioned tent beside his hacienda home on the 50 thousand acre ranch. My act was quite well-received, like any other date of its kind, and Frank Yturria was very happy. He thanked me and said we should get together again the next time I played the Palm Springs Follies. At the time, I had no idea where that chance encounter would lead in the future.

November through May, the Follies played to sold-out audiences. They all came to see me, family members, old friends, and ghosts from the past. I was asked to perform for an Academy Awards banquet, and Bob Hope's wife, Dolores, sent a message that read, "That's the funniest act I've ever seen." I wondered if that also included her husband's…. Movie stars, television stars, and sports celebrities came and saw me perform with Francisco. I was offered a lot of work from having been seen in the Follies. The eight-month season ended in the last week of May, and before I left Palm Springs, Francisco and I had a contract to return for the 12th season of the show beginning November, 2002.

Between closing at the Follies that season and reopening a year and a half later, there were months of cruise ships in the Caribbean, down the Mexican coast, and to Alaska, India, and Africa. It was not a bad life, but cruising didn't suit my appetite for being on stage every night instead of just once or twice a week, and gone were the days of boarding and disembarking in the same U.S. port. New policies required all entertainers coming on board to fly long distances to foreign countries and wait for the ship to dock, board mid-cruise, and perform several shows throughout the remainder of the cruise. Then, when the ship docked, the acts were to remain on board as the ship set sail with a new group of passengers and, again, perform several shows before disembarking mid-cruise and flying home from another distant port. I encountered many problems with these new rules. In addition to dealing with customs and immigration in foreign ports, I experienced lost luggage and missing props on more than one occasion, and I also found it difficult to share passenger enthusiasm or bond with the crew because I didn't fit in with either group.

I also worked a few weeks in Las Vegas at the Hotel San Remo in *Show Girls of Magic* and in *Melinda, First Lady of Magic* at the Venetian. Then, I received a request for a production in Ohio from a producer who had seen me in the Follies. The Carousel Dinner Theatre in Akron, Ohio, had a Las Vegas-type production show lasting four months each year. Although the show was scheduled for the Christmas season, the offer unfortunately came at a time of turmoil in our country, September 11, 2001. The production was a children's show on Sunday afternoons, and I was playing an old toy maker using a hand puppet of a tiny jester doing my Teddy bit. Juggler, Nino Frediani, was also booked, so he and I shared an apartment for the run of the show. During that time, I met and visited with Ken Groves, one of the most proficient ventriloquists in the art of speaking the difficult letters, B, M, and P, without a trace of lip movement.

That summer, I attended the ventriloquist conVENTion in Fort Mitchell, Kentucky, and, at the Vent Haven Museum, I caught up with some of the more famous ventriloquists of the times. I also got to know some of the ventriloquists who regularly performed at schools, libraries, corporate events, and comedy clubs. I had never met most of them because I was always booked somewhere, but, to be sure, I was amazed at how many of them knew my act. Some were amateurs, some were professionals, but all of them shared the knowledge and love of ventriloquism, and, to me, that was something I could not find in others around the world.

After Ohio, I returned to cabarets in Las Vegas, Casino Arizona in Phoenix, corporate engagements in Los Angeles, and an occasional cruise ship or comedy club in Houston, Texas, until it was time to return to Palm Springs for a long run in the Follies once again.

The Fabulous Palm Springs Follies
Season XII, 2002-2003

Opening in my second season at the Follies was much easier for me, having appeared there before. I was already familiar with the town, the theater, the show's rules of conduct, and the rest of the cast. Rehearsals started in September for the November opening, but the acts were all self-contained and didn't need to arrive in Palm Springs until approximately 10 days prior to the first performance. However, in addition to doing my act in the program, I was to play a part in the extensive opening number entitled "Flying Down to Rio." The number had a Brazilian setting, and there was a nightclub scene where I was seated at a table with Francisco perched next to me. We were watching the floor show, and, as the spotlight hit us, Francisco was to deliver his line. I was dressed in a colorful lime green and orange costume and wearing a sombrero. My face was on the table, and I was pretending to be asleep during the entire number, while Francisco was actively looking in every direction, watching and reacting to the action on stage. Since I could not "see" what was going on around me, I had to memorize all the staging and choreography. This was another first in my professional career, and, because the entire opening number was quite long, there was much direction involved. When the music finally stopped at the end of the number, Francisco was the focus of the entire cast as he made the introduction, "Ladies and Gentlemen, the managing director of The Fabulous Palm Springs Follies...Mr. Riff Markowitz." Then, Mr. Markowitz would make his grand entrance down the center stairs and past the table where I was sitting and Francisco was "squawking." This small, simple bit took all 10 days of rehearsal to get it right, and we finally had to pre-record the announcement for Francisco to lip sync, or beak sync, the words. With the sombrero covering my face on the table, there was a tendency to over-relax and doze off, causing my hand inside Francisco to "doze" as well. After a few weeks into the show, I actually fell asleep and, unfortunately, Francisco fell over in the process.

Because I was a returning engagement act that season, there was an entertainment writer from a local publication sent to interview me one day in my dressing room. I wasn't told about the interview beforehand and only learned of it when I arrived at the show for the first matinee. Needless to say, I was not prepared and had to "wing" my way through the question and answer session. To see the interview in its entirety, please see Appendix C: The Interview.

Another memorable incident from Follies XII was seeing my fellow vent, Jay Johnson, again; however, Jay and his wife, Sandi, were not at the show to see me. They were there to watch Sandi's mother, Maxine, one of the dancers in the cast. Maxine was an alert and energetic woman, well into her years, a very good dancer, and quite the driver. Once, when juggler, Nino Frediani, and I were driving to Las Vegas during a couple of days off from the show, Maxine asked if she could follow us from Palm Springs to Interstate 15 because she wasn't familiar with the directions. I drove at a speed limit of 70 miles per hour, and, when we got to the highway intersection leading to Vegas, Maxine passed me doing more than 85 miles per hour! When we all got back to Palm Springs, I called her "Lead Foot" for the rest of the season.

During season XII of the Follies, I got another phone call from Frank Yturria wanting to know if we could meet again, this time at his winter home located in nearby Indian Wells at the El Dorado Country Club Estates. So, on one of my days off from the show, we visited for awhile and, then, went out to dinner at a very posh restaurant. He told me of his next party; a combination 80th birthday and 60th anniversary affair. I agreed to do it, and, after discussing the event, I asked him if I could produce all of the entertainment including the orchestra, acts, and even a 20-minute video of his life together with his wife. Frank agreed, and, with a budget that was befitting a first-class event, I started gathering memorable photographs and video footage of his life. To my surprise, I learned that Mr. Yturria's friends included the governor of Texas, Rick Perry, and actor, Tommy Lee Jones, among other well-known names. He had an extensive photo collection of himself with Roy Rogers, Gene Autry, Noel Coward, Nelson Rockefeller, and Presidents Gerald Ford, Richard Nixon, Ronald Reagan, George H. W. Bush, and George W. Bush. It was obvious that Frank Yturria's life had crossed paths with some very high profile persons.

I spent most of the next four months putting together a video of Frank and Mary's life over a 60-year period. It consisted of music and pictures from six decades along with some footage of their ranch and incorporating some animal conservation videos. The show itself would have six acts, a 12-piece orchestra from Las Vegas, and the video. The show, a black tie affair, was held at the country club in Brownsville, Texas, (which also allowed me to attend my 50th high school class reunion while in town), and my hard work was well-rewarded. The party was a huge success, and I knew I had not seen the last of Frank Yturria.

The Follies season closed for the summer months, but I wasn't too concerned because I was already committed for future work at the Casino Arizona in Phoenix. It's not that I didn't need a break, but I simply never liked the idea of being away from the stage for very long, so, when the phone rang, I was on my way to Florida. Now, when any show is a huge success, there will inevitably be knock-offs, or copies, and such was the case with the Fort Lauderdale Follies. Given the number of retirement communities in the area, there was motivation to do a Follies-type production show. Similar in format to the Palm Springs Follies in California, the Florida version was hosted by Florence Henderson of The Brady Bunch fame. In addition to Ms. Henderson, the two-hour program featured comedians, Jack Carter and Norm Crosby. The cast was also older because it made good copy for the press, and it was the nature of the show. Southern Florida had many semi-retired celebrities in residence, working the plentiful condo circuit. The show's contract was open-ended, which, to me, meant indefinite and subject to two week's notice.

Attendance at the Fort Lauderdale Follies was only average, even though the winter season brought snowbirds from places up north, but, for some reason, they didn't flock to the show. After three months of small audiences, the show closed, sending the cast packing. Again, I was faced with filling in some open weeks before returning to my favorite showroom at Casino Arizona. So, it was back to the Coachella Valley (Palm Springs) for a couple of private parties and a chance to play the McCallum Theatre as the opening act for Joel Grey. As a youth, I had memorized several cuts from an album by his father, Mickey Katz, a Yiddish comedian. I would later convert one of Mr. Katz's bits into a story told by my Poppa figure called "How the Jewish People Helped Win the West."

The Fabulous Palm Springs Follies
Season XIV, 2004-2005

The Follies season XII had come and gone, resulting in an amazing number of extra bookings for me, all from being seen in Palm Springs. My contract read that I was not allowed to work on days or nights off within 100 miles of Palm Springs. Still, I did quite a few well-paid dates outside the restricted radius. At the end of the run, I had a contract to play one year at a Native American casino in Turtle Lake, Wisconsin. It was a very big production with a 12-piece band conducted by Al Capone's grandson and two magicians: Bruce Block's comedy magic and James Dimmare, the Fred Astaire look-a-like magician from the old Bahamas show. Dancers were staged and choreographed by Bonnie Saxe, whose daughter, Mindy, was known in Las Vegas as *Melinda, the First Lady of Magic*. Bonnie was a dancer earlier in her career at the Tropicana's *Folies Bergere*, and her daughter, Suzanne, was also a dancer and singer. Her son, David, was a successful Vegas show producer, and I had shared the stage with all of them at one time, or another, in various Las Vegas shows.

The show in Wisconsin should have enjoyed a long run, but there were unforeseen circumstances that caused it to become the second shortest production in my career. Produced by Jerry Schafer, the show opened to a sold-out invited audience, but, thereafter, drew very few paying customers. Turtle Lake was at the crossroads on a Native American reservation, visited mostly by travelers from the road and truckers making a rest stop. The tribe was in the process of changing chairmen, and, apparently, the new management was not too interested in promoting a Vegas-type show. With very poor attendance, the production closed at the end of the first week, and I quickly took other work, splitting my weeks between Phoenix and Las Vegas over the next five months. In addition, I once again worked on cruise ships for Royal Caribbean with cruises to Alaska, Mexico, and the Caribbean.

At the time, cruise ships were still booking name acts along with an opening act spot doing about 20 minutes. So, as an opener, I could use both Francisco and Teddy, play guitar, and even do some stand-up comedy. I opened for comedian, David Brenner; impressionist, Frank Gorshin; and Broadway star, Carol Lawrence. At that time, Carol was a singer, actress, and dancer whose role as Maria in *West Side Story* earned her a Tony award nomination. I met Carol during my second season in the Palm Springs Follies when singer/dancer Randy Doney, (who danced eleven years on *The Carol Burnett Show*), invited the cast of the Follies to his house for a home-cooked Italian dinner prepared by Ms. Lawrence. The multi-talented Mr. Doney was a surprisingly good classical pianist with a knack for comedy, and, along with his youthful good looks, was a marvelous stage performer.

My third season at the Follies was much like the first two seasons. I was given a first-class condominium near the Plaza Theatre with perks, like having my wardrobe taken to the dry cleaner at the end of every week and a dresser to escort me from my dressing room to the stage area five minutes before my entrance. In that season XIV, my escort was Elizabeth "Beth" Bendgen, a quiet, unassuming, but very professional dresser who also loved popcorn. I mention that fact because she always made sure there were two large bowls of popcorn in the green room for every show, one for the cast and one for the crew. But, more importantly, Elizabeth was to become my companion on and off stage for the next 10+ years.

As in previous seasons, the list of Follies stars once again included Tony Martin, Julius LaRosa, Susan Anton, The Four Aces, Donald O'Connor, Howard Keel, John Davidson, and Kaye Ballard. I had once opened for Kaye Ballard at the famous Coconut Grove in the Ambassador Hotel in Los Angeles. Kaye was a wonderful performer who told hilarious stories, both on and off stage. She invited me for dinner at her home, once owned by Lucille Ball and Desi Arnaz, in nearby Rancho Mirage. The home had a museum-like history in photographs, and it was located on Kaye Ballard Lane.

In addition to the marquee headliners, there were also first-rate variety acts, such as vaudeville's Mercer Brothers; magician "Mr. Electric," Marvyn Roy; burlesque star, Tempest Storm; plate spinner, Leonardo; and my old juggler friend, Nino Frediani, just to name a few. All cast members of the Follies had very distinguished careers and were still performing well into their twilight years. There were also many names in the Follies with whom I had previously crossed paths during my career. One member was Wayne Albritton, who had a career in New York and Las Vegas as a dancer with Ann-Margaret. Wayne was married to Greta, a dancer with whom I had worked in Matt Gregory's *Fancy That* 30 years earlier in Reno and in *Lance Burton's Magic Show* at the Hacienda Hotel in Vegas. The dance captain, Jill Owens, was someone I had watched perform in *Pippin* on Broadway. Glenda Guilfoyle was a former dancer in the *Golden Horseshoe Revue* at Disneyland and, later, on the *The Dean Martin Show* and in the movie version of *The Music Man*. Judy Bell was a Vegas lounge star whose show had played often at the Dunes Hotel during my run with *Vive Les Girls* in the 1960s.

During the season, I received another call and visit from Frank Yturria to talk about celebrating his 85th birthday with yet another party at the country club in Brownsville. This one, however, was a much smaller event as many of his old cronies were either dead or too ill to attend. Along with my act, he wanted me to contract either Steve Tyrell or Jack Jones to sing and Johnny Lonestar, the trick roper who had done the previous gala. Neither Tyrell nor Jones was available, so Mr. Yturria's next request was for impressionist, Rich Little. I had worked at the Nugget as an opening act for Rich and called to see if he was available. He was, and I sent him a contract with a 50% deposit to secure the date. We performed the show to about 150 party guests, and, again, it was a successful event. I was learning the ropes of producing a show – hiring musicians and stage technicians, handling sound and lighting equipment, and making travel arrangements and accommodations. I thought this might be my future in the business, but, as fate would have it, there were life changes coming.

Before season XIV closed, I was offered another contract to return for an unprecedented fourth year in Follies XVI. Interestingly, though, I had been seen at the Plaza Theatre by Andy Williams, who had his own Moon River Theatre in Branson, Missouri – yes, the same Branson that had once canceled me – and he invited me to come back there.

After closing that third season with the Follies, and before traveling to Branson, Jerry Schaffer called and asked if I would be interested in joining a new show he was opening in Las Vegas. I felt bad about Jerry's tough luck with the show in Turtle Lake, Wisconsin, but believed he was an honorable man. He had paid me two weeks salary when the show closed suddenly, so I asked him some details about his new show, all which sounded rather curious. It was not on the Strip, but at a theater located in the small Chinatown section of Vegas. The show, called *No MSG*, featured a live band, dancers, and a Chinese acrobat troupe. When I arrived, the showroom was still in the construction process. There were problems with some of the Vegas unions that had backed the opening. For example, a handicap ramp leading up to the stage was required even though no one in the cast was physically challenged.

Jerry Schaffer's two assistants were a couple of Chinese ladies he nicknamed Ping and Pong. In addition to a singer who was billed as "A Diamond in the Rough," the show also included juggler, Romano Frediani, the son of Nino Frediani, my co-worker from the Palm Springs Follies and the Carousel Dinner Theater in Akron, Ohio. While legally blind, Nino was billed as one of the world's fastest jugglers. Romano was doing a version of his father's act and doing it quite well. But, while he was warming up with soccer balls just before my act was to go on, one of the balls sailed over the sectioned-off dressing room, knocking down all my props and the makeshift fan and lighting. It all came crashing down just as Ping, or Pong, knocked on the door to tell me I was due on stage. That, in itself, was memorable, but not nearly as much as the five people who comprised the audience waiting for my entrance.

The following day, I asked about getting a phone installed in the apartment provided for me as part of the contract. "First, read letter," was what Ping, or Pong, kept trying to tell me in her Chinese-English accent. The letter was a notice that the show was closing immediately – there was no two-week, or even two-day, advance notice! We had, apparently, just done our last show an hour earlier to 12 Chinese tourists in Las Vegas.

I was on my way to Branson, Missouri...

Return to Branson

The first time I saw Branson in the rear view mirror of my truck, I thought it would also be my last. Having just closed The Fabulous Palm Springs Follies, season XIV, two days before, I was to play Casino Arizona in Phoenix for two weeks, and, then, I was focused on settling back into the now "new" Las Vegas. I packed my props, clothes, and personal effects into my truck and drove to Arizona. Arriving in Scottsdale about 3:30am, I locked the truck and went inside to bed. The next morning, I went outside to start unloading my things only to discover that my truck was gone. At first, I questioned whether, or not, I had forgotten where I parked, but I soon realized I had been robbed. Everything was gone – my only remaining possessions were the toothbrush, pajamas, and change of clothes I had taken inside with me. And, when I say everything was gone, I mean EVERYTHING. Francisco, props, two guitars, videos, and my clothes were all in the truck and camper shell I had just purchased a couple weeks earlier in Palm Springs. I called the police first, (they sent an officer a couple of hours later to record my story), and, then, I called Gregg Austin, the producer of the show, to explain why I would not be opening that night. Twice before in my career, I had my props separated from me on airline flights; once, in Miami, while waiting to board a cruise ship and, then, another time when I arrived in Puerto Rico and my prop case went to South Africa and didn't come back for two months. But, this time, everything was stolen, not lost, and it was not coming back. I kept imagining that somewhere just a few miles away, south of the Arizona border, Francisco was "at home" in Mexico and some mariachi was dressed in a tailor-made tuxedo playing my very expensive handmade Spanish guitar.

I had left a few things in storage in Palm Springs, including the previous Francisco. It was usually my routine to build a new Francisco whenever I had a long run anywhere. Being a soft puppet, the feathers were marabou boas that would generally last through about 500 shows before fading or losing their fluffiness. In 50 years of performing, I had built 35 different versions of the puppet, each a little different and better than the last. The problem, though, was that I usually transferred something from the former model to the new one, and, in this case, it was the eyes. So, the last one was pretty much either torn apart or rendered non-repairable, as was the case with Francisco model #34. I drove a rented car back to Palm Springs to retrieve what was left of my stored belongings, and, after assessing my situation, I had no choice but to build another Francisco. But, old #34 was useless, and it took me about 24 hours to complete #35 – the quickest turnaround time yet!

Casino Arizona in Phoenix had a mini-Vegas showroom that, in addition to marquee acts, was home to an impressionist show similar to *Legends in Concert* with dancers and musical acts. The show, named *Showstoppers Live*, was enjoying a 10-year run and featured a comedy act. It was also one of the few shows left with a live band, which allowed my act's music to meet the changing energy of each audience. I would appear in the show during my "down time," typically about 12 to 20 weeks a year, and, whenever my daughter, Kristi, danced in the show, I proudly shared the stage with her. If I was appearing during the Christmas season, Francisco would sing a version of Jose Feliciano's "Feliz Navidad," and I would add some fitting Christmas/Hanukkah material.

The format at *Showstoppers Live* was flexible for whenever acts wanted to change, or cancel, weeks of engagement. Once, I needed a two-week leave to do another date, and I recommended Dan Horn as my replacement. Dan's control rod manipulation of his puppets was legendary in ventriloquist circles, and I always considered his work remarkable and his act outstanding. When I first returned from Paris, I had often watched Dan on local television in Phoenix. He was currently a regular on the after-school program, *The Wallace and Ladmo Show*, performing four, or five, different short bits a week. I was sure Dan's name and characters would be easily recognizable because of his long run in town, but, apparently, not many of the show's fans frequented Casino Arizona. The feedback confirmed that Francisco was the preferred bird in the showroom, and, apparently, he was a tough act to follow.

When I finished in Phoenix, I moved into my daughter Kristi's new house in Las Vegas. She was working day and night in two different hotels, a grind for sure, but, then, she was 18 and very talented. My older daughter, Alicia, and her husband, Neal, tried to move to Las Vegas, as well; but, after a couple months of trying to make the transition from theater in Colorado to the club scene in Nevada, they returned to the Boulder Dinner Theatre to continue their musical theater careers. It would have been great to work in Las Vegas with both my girls nearby, but it was not to be…

I was on my way back to Missouri, based on that phone call from Andy Williams offering me a spot in the Christmas show at his theater in Branson. I admit I had hesitated, hearing "Branson" and remembering my history, but, when he offered to pay me a handsome salary and said I could do my act exactly as I did it in the Palm Springs Follies, I agreed to the contract. Having seen so many of Andy's Christmas shows on television over the years, I knew it would be another notch on my "performing belt." The show was opening in November, so I had six months to prepare. When the contract arrived, I discovered there was a paragraph stating I would do two spots in the show. I immediately thought to revive Teddy's bit, but change some of the script to adapt more to Branson's Baptist Bible Belt acceptability standards.

I had already booked a few more weeks in *Showstoppers Live* at Casino Arizona, and I thought I could break in the new material there. But, then, I decided to create a whole new second act with Francisco using some animatronics instead. However, that decision would require building another puppet duplicating the same look, but adding some remote control gimmicks. I had done this once before in Paris with the shaking cage and flying feathers, but, this time, it was going to be a flicking tail and fluttering wings. In addition to those new movements, Francisco's perch would have a water bowl on one side and a seed bowl on the other. At one strategic point in the act, he would be "eating" sunflower seeds making chewing noises while I was speaking to the audience. I would accomplish this by my left hand crunching a simple piece of plastic bottle in time with Francisco's beak motion. Then, after a long, slow, disapproving look from me, he would "gulp" and take a drink of water, gargle for a couple of seconds, and swallow with a final smacking "ah" sound.

I was also looking forward to summer and the annual ventriloquist conVENTion at Vent Haven in Fort Mitchell, Kentucky. It was always an educational experience as well as an enjoyable reunion of friends and fellow performers, both amateur and pro. Francisco and I had made some limited appearances over the years, both at Vent Haven and at the International Vent Event in Las Vegas, and I was very happy to be available for this year's get-to-

From left to right: Brad Cummings, Jimmy Nelson, Jeff Dunham, and Sammy King at Vent Haven Museum

gether.

For the remaining five months, I split my weeks between Casino Arizona's *Showstoppers Live* and Planet Hollywood's *V* (the ultimate variety show) until it was time to drive across the country back to Branson; however, this time I was less sure of myself, Francisco's new act, and the yet unknown possible derailments awaiting us.

Three days after leaving Las Vegas, I drove into Branson and entered the Moon River Theatre in the middle of Andy Williams' rehearsal. His orchestra was on stage along with several backup singers, all surrounded by a Christmas setting. It was a beautiful 2,000-seat theater with possibly the best state-of-the-art sound system I had ever heard. The dressing room was first-class with a bar, stocked refrigerator, bathroom, lounging area, and a TV monitor of the stage happenings. The tap dancing Williams Brothers (no relation to Andy) were another act in the show, and we shared the spacious dressing room. After dropping off my show props and wardrobe, I was given a rehearsal schedule and directions to the condominium provided for the run of the show. I was thinking "so far, so good," and since I was not due to rehearse until the following day, I thought I had ample time to rediscover the town where I was canceled years before with Lee Greenwood. However, Branson's Highway 76 was the strip where most of the theaters were located, side by side, one after another for a couple of miles, and, although it was officially the off-season, cars were lined up, bumper to bumper, and creeping along at a snail's pace. I didn't get very far in my rediscovery.

The following day at the scheduled rehearsal, I was told that the length of the show was way over the planned running time, and, therefore, I would only be able to do one spot with Francisco. I had mixed feelings, having spent so much time creating a second act for the show, but, at the same time, I was somewhat relieved that I would not have to experiment with something yet unproven. Life was good and getting better by the hour. The orchestra, conducted by the very capable Joe Galante, was spot-on with my music and even the play-on and chaser were outstanding. My rehearsal took all of 20 minutes, and we were done, except for some lighting cues for the crew. Sitting in the theater watching the rest of the show rehearsing, my confidence was high, and, when the cast took a dinner break, I became even more certain that all was going to be just as I had hoped. There was one final complete run through, and everyone left for the night. The first show would be a matinee the following day, but, as it turned out, not for me!

94

Two hours before it was time to leave for the theater, I blew my nose into a kleenex, and it started bleeding. It kept bleeding, and I tried everything I knew to make it stop. Leaning my head back, applying pressure, an ice pack, and even a styptic pencil couldn't stop the flow of blood that seemed to rival the Red River back in Texas. I called the stage manager and explained my dilemma, and he suggested I come to the theater anyway, saying it would probably stop soon, but it never did. I imagined that a tourniquet around my neck might be a solution, but, at the time, it was no laughing matter. At a half an hour before show time, Andy Williams was advised of my situation and simply said that I should be taken to the hospital. The show opened without Sammy King and Francisco. It was yet another first in my career, and I was wondering if Branson was giving me a message.

At Skaggs hospital, I had the blood vessel in my nose cauterized and recovered in time for the evening performance. There was not much talk about my nosebleed, as everyone, including Andy Williams, was preoccupied with their own part in the show. So, I nervously did my first act and received a very good reaction, all things considered. After a few weeks of successful performances, I was interested in seeing some of the other shows in town, including another knock-off of the Palm Springs Follies. This one starred John Byner, The Four Aces, and, of course, a line of long-legged lovelies whose age alone was the novelty of the show. I attended a performance on the showboat, Branson Belle, and saw ventriloquist, Todd Oliver, a long-time Branson favorite with his talking dogs. Jim Barber was another great ventriloquist in town for a number of years at the Hamner Barber Theater, starring with magician, Dave Hamner, in a very successful show.

The Andy Williams Christmas production closed mid-December, and the entire cast traveled with Andy on his annual multi-city holiday season tour before returning to Branson after the New Year. At that point, I thought it might be a good idea to remain in Branson for a while. Johnny Lonestar, the trick roper from *Country Tonite* in Las Vegas was a regular in *Clay Cooper's Country Music Express* at the Caravelle Theatre, and he introduced me to Clay Cooper for a trial audition. I was hired and began a steady run of good shows. And, just about the time I decided Branson was being good to me, I had the biggest setback of my career – a heart attack.

Serious as a Heart Attack
Memorial Day, 2006
Houston, Texas

At first, I thought it was indigestion. Then, I thought I had eaten too much hot salsa or much too hot a salsa. So, I excused myself a couple times from my uncle's invited guests at the festive dining table and laid down (big mistake). When I finally surrendered to the fact that something was wrong, I said, "Call 911." It was the first time I had ever said those words, and it was also my first great heart pain, other than all the emotional ones I had suffered since being rejected at a Junior High School dance. The ambulance ride was rather musical as I lay there recalling my first night in Lance Burton's Magic Show at the Hacienda Hotel in Las Vegas when a fire alarm went off accidentally and sounded throughout my entire time on stage.

By the time the ambulance reached the North Houston Hospital, I could no longer hear the siren or the paramedic who had said, "I don't know if this guy is going to make it." All I could "see" at the time was an indigo blue light with thousands of stars in a series of weird dreams and nightmares. It was a euphoric feeling, painless, and possibly even pleasurable. Some of my dreams were those of performing with the six characters I had created: Teddy, Francisco, Rojo, Henrietta, Buckaroo Buddy, and Poppa, and, in my dreams, I was a great ventriloquist. I would later learn that I had suffered a massive heart attack and slipped into a comatose state lasting for several months.

During those weeks and months in the coma, my daughters, ex-wives in the area, brothers, and cousins all came to visit, and I wondered what they were all doing in Texas. Some were talking of "pulling the plug," thinking I might never be happy with the quality of life that had taken over and asking why should they let me lie there suffering? I didn't understand because I wasn't in pain, and I certainly wasn't suffering, probably due to all the prescription drugs in my system. After almost 100 days, I finally opened my eyes and tried to speak. Nothing came out – not a sound. "How will I do my act" was my first thought. Being unable to speak was causing me to get somewhat violent, and I was constantly trying to rip the intubation out of my throat, so I was restrained at the wrists and ankles.

I remained in the intensive care ward long enough to experience Sundowners Syndrome, which was extremely taxing and stressful. Doctors aren't sure what causes sundowning, but the symptoms are confusion and agitation as the sun goes down. Sure enough, I feared the dark and lost track of time. I had to have either AM or PM put under the clock on the hospital wall because I felt completely lost not knowing if it was day or night. The agitation and confusion that lasted throughout the nights kept me from sleeping, and, if I did fall asleep, I was constantly having that show business nightmare of being late for the show, adding more stress (the real killer) to my daily hospital life.

Being intubated for such a long period of time had permanently scarred my vocal cords. In addition, I could barely move my fingers, let alone my hands and arms. Relatives, friends, even strangers were in and out of my hospital room, and I was unable to do much more than blink, think, and cry out in frustration. The lyrics to hundreds of songs I had played came to mind as I lay in bed, "Oh, Mama, can this really be the end?" Then, Teddy's voice would come to mind with his blunt advice, "Stop with all the drama," so I thought I could cheer myself up by trying to dance to an internal conversation about my life, but nothing was funny anymore. I never could dance, but I could always make dancers laugh by trying. How ironic to have spent a lifetime sharing stages and dressing rooms with hundreds of beautiful, laughing singers and dancers.

When I was finally allowed to go outside in a wheelchair to breathe fresh air for brief periods of time, I fought returning indoors. At one point, I got out of the chair and rolled in the grass just outside the hospital entrance. The prognosis was not good, and I could not think long-term anymore. Viewing any videos, or even watching television, was depressing and made the time go by much more slowly. When I asked about the tube in my neck, the answer was always that I would probably have to live with it, and, if I asked for an explanation, I was answered in medical terms I couldn't understand; "Studies have shown that the result of mechanical dilation may incur a high mortality rate and/or a rate of recurrences of stenosis, which could be treated by endoscopic excision dilation and prolonged stenting with a silicone T-tube." Blah, Blah, Blah…. But, what about venting? Will I ever be able to do that again? No one could answer that inquiry. Given my condition at the time, there was no help available.

Physical Therapy, Recovery, Discovery, and Depression

I left the hospital in Houston after many long and difficult physical therapy sessions. My first six steps with a walker had been a miracle in itself. Then, eight steps, ten steps, and so on. It was going to be a long recovery period before I could speak and walk again, let alone perform on stage, or so I was told by numerous doctors and surgeons. I refused to accept that diagnosis. So, with Elizabeth continually changing the nasty T-tube in my throat for breathing and pushing me in my wheelchair, we left Houston and drove back to Branson.

When I could walk far enough to reach a microphone from the stage wings, I tried my best to get back on stage in Clay Cooper's show. It was way too soon, and I failed miserably, but I continued to push myself so hard that I ended up in the hospital with congestive heart failure, this time at Branson's Skagg's Hospital. Clay and a few other fellow entertainers came to visit me there, and, to my amazement, so did Andy Williams. His kindness was very touching to me, especially considering the fact that I was no longer in his show. However, I was becoming very depressed at the thought of barely being able to breathe, let alone do ventriloquism. I remember wanting to say good-bye to life more than a few times. I felt that if I could no longer be on stage, I didn't know where I fit into the world. Looking back, I am amazed that Elizabeth stayed with all I put her through. I was not only in ill health; I was difficult to be around, too. When the doctors explained that I was, once again, experiencing Sundowners Syndrome, my actions finally made sense to Elizabeth, but I just felt more upset and unhappy with my situation.

At times, I argued with myself in two characters, as one might imagine would be normal for a ventriloquist, but my doctors all agreed that I needed some psychiatric care. A psychiatrist was sent in to talk to me, and, when he left the hospital room where I had acted quite normally, he believed there was absolutely nothing wrong or unusual. But, then, within minutes, it would all turn around again, and I couldn't escape the feeling of being lost without a stage, a microphone, and an audience. It was like hell on earth for me there in Branson.

Elizabeth and I left the Ozarks and drove back to California where I would start on the road to recovery. My windpipe had curved as a result of healing with that tube in my throat for such a long time. It's U-shape allowed very little air to pass over my severely damaged vocal cords, or what was left of them. I started the long process of looking for a surgeon to operate and resection my windpipe by removing the couple of inches that was curved and had closed down to half its proper diameter; however, I had no luck finding anyone willing to try the procedure.

My continuous search for a throat surgeon was exhausting. Inquiries at the Mayo Clinic, Cedars-Sinai, Cleveland Clinic, and even the Veteran's Hospital in Loma Linda, California, would all say the same thing; because of my heart condition, there was nothing that could be done about the tracheal stenosis that was keeping me from getting back on stage as a ventriloquist. My active travels and desperate search for a cure combined with my several congestive heart failure episodes throughout Missouri, Arizona, California, and Nevada had caused setbacks and further damage to my heart, as well. And, the days and weeks I spent in one place, or another, had only served as a reminder of times and places long past. I no longer thought about all the audience applause while taking bows or the calls of "Bravo" in European cabarets. I could only recall all the times when there was some sort of derailment that kept me from doing the act perfectly.

The Last Folly

Over the next couple of years, I would try, again and again, to return to the stage only to fail at the one thing I did best in life – ventriloquism. Though I fought beyond my abilities, first in Branson, then, again in Phoenix, and, finally, back in the Palm Springs Follies, I was falling deeper into a darkness I had never known before: physically, emotionally, and spiritually.

Tracheal stenosis was getting in my way physically. Without my ventriloquial technique, I was certainly not able to "throw my voice" anymore, and I couldn't even apply any of the lessons I had been teaching others for 20 years. The biggest problem was that I barely had three tone pitches, all close together, so I could not project two different sounding voices. In addition, with every inhale, I was making a horrible sound that not only kept me from getting enough oxygen, but also became amplified by the microphone. I started experimenting with different techniques, like turning my head with every breath to squash the sounds I was scraping out, but that threw my timing way off, and, as any comedic actor knows; the secret to comedy _is_ TIMING.

At Casino Arizona, where I first returned in a wheelchair, it was depressing to be seen and heard doing the act so differently. Then, there was one more trip to another hospital with cardiac arrest, this time at the Mayo Clinic. I was actually becoming the proverbial clown, laughing on the outside and crying on the inside. But, enough pity! Over-medicated on prescription drugs and faking my well-being, I vowed to return to the stage. But, once back on stage, I had to hide my capped breathing tube under a wing-tipped tuxedo shirt. Then, in the middle of Francisco's act, the cap popped out, which meant there was absolutely no voice coming out of my mouth – my ultimate fear. The sound of wheezing was all I could muster. I couldn't even excuse myself. After two or three seconds of silence (a lifetime on stage), trying with only my left hand to plug in the dangling cap under my shirt, I just walked off stage without saying a word, yet another first in my now dwindling career.

"Why, God, why" I asked, already knowing the answer. The future expectations I was given by doctors in reply to so many health questions were not what I wanted to hear. I would record myself, then, listen with so much disappointment. Francisco sounded pathetic. His voice was worse

Sammy King and Poppa

than mine, so I turned to Teddy's now graveled voice and convinced myself it sounded better that way. He was 70 years old in dummy years, (figuratively speaking), and his "Buckaroo Buddy" Texas drawl a palaver that made sense for an old cowboy. And, Poppa came into being as an old, thick-accented Jewish storyteller. But, how could my figures be funny if they couldn't even be understood? The best sound I could produce was by cocking my head to one side and slightly stretching out my curved windpipe. It looked stupid.

I had signed another contract to play the Follies in Palm Springs, but that had to be put off for another season during which time ventriloquist, Brad Cummings, and his lovable dinosaur puppet, Rex, became the new Follies hit. I had been Brad's mentor, going back to my season in Puerto Rico some 20 years earlier, and he had also done some Fredric Apcar productions in Reno and Tahoe about a decade after me. His act was ideally the right amount of time and energy needed for the Follies' audiences, and, maybe, even better than mine.

Meanwhile, I continued making trips to various throat surgeons to evaluate my options. In all, I consulted doctors at seven major clinics. The answers were all the same – with 65% of my heart dead and gone forever, I was stuck with my condition. Repairing my damaged vocal cords was not an option because the procedure would take longer than my heart could handle. Then, in the last place I thought I would find a medical possibility, Dr. Robert Wang, a throat surgeon teaching at the University of Nevada, Las Vegas Medical, was my last hope. He had created a technique to repair tracheas and had treated a few patients with moderate success. It was not the usual "cut and resection" procedure, but a simple balloon put in place to blow out the collapsed windpipe. The technique minimized the amount of operating time under anesthesia, and it would give me a 50/50 chance of survival. If successful, the amount of waiting time was about three months, and, if my trachea didn't collapse by then, I was "home free." However, at eleven weeks, the attempt failed, and I was turning blue and gasping for air once again.

Dr. Wang was reluctant to try the procedure again, but I was more than willing. As I was being prepped for the operation, I was surprisingly calm and confident. When it was over, there was a problem bringing me out of anesthesia, and Dr. Wang was relieved when I came around. "I was very concerned, even nervous. I thought I had lost you," he said later. Now, it was just a matter of waiting another three months. This time, the surgery was successful, and the wind pipe remained "blown-out." I was even able to do a limited amount of ventriloquism, although not nearly as well as before. So, unable to perform, I wanted to get away from friends and relatives in Las Vegas. A trip to Colorado seemed like a good idea. I felt that a little time with my granddaughter, Samantha Prugh Dunfee, would surely help me put doctors and hospitals behind me.

The altitude in Denver, the mile high city, made it necessary for me to tote around an oxygen tank, which, while a safety precaution, was also a constant reminder that nothing was the same. I tried to shake off any negative thoughts by getting back on stage, prematurely, at Lannie's Clocktower Cabaret in downtown Denver. The show was a modern day burlesque revue that featured exotic dancers and a couple of variety acts. It took me back to the 1960s when I worked as a master of ceremonies and comedian between strippers. The most difficult part of performing in Denver's thin air was finding new breathing spaces in Francisco's once rapid-fire script. Where I used to do up to eight lines of patter back and forth before needing to inhale, I now found myself out of breath at every other line. My inhales were sounding as loud as my voice, and I would have to turn my head to the side to keep from being heard with every breath. My timing was way off, and the once funny lines were now getting less than half the response of years past.

Mark Hellerstein's home in Colorado had always been a refreshing and constructive visit for me. Over the 20 years since I had first started coaching him, writing his scripts, and building his props, we had not only established a friendship, but he was my most dedicated student of the stage. We even did a bilingual children's show together at a theater in Denver where I used an old Francisco puppet I had donated to his fine collection of ventriloquist figures. His museum-like display of dummies in a perfect setting, complete with a stage and lights, was a playground, and we spent many hours recording sessions to improve his numerous acts.

Staying with my daughter, Alicia, and her husband in nearby Lyons and taking morning walks with my granddaughter seemed to be just what I needed until one night when I woke up with excruciating abdominal pains. I had a mild heart attack while visiting there once before and thought I had been a little too hasty in going to the hospital, so I waited and monitored my condition for a while this time. After a few hours, when I could no longer take the pain, I woke my daughter at 4:00am for another emergency call. The half hour drive from Lyons to Boulder Community Hospital seemed much longer as my pains grew stronger, and I thought I might not make it when we finally reached the Emergency Room. I had my infected gall bladder removed, and, after a couple weeks of rest and recuperation, I returned to Palm Springs.

My medical issues finally seemed behind me until lab work at a doctor appointment showed traces of blood in my urine. My cardiologist referred me to an Urologist for a basic evaluation. "Here we go again," I thought, and, as sure as the sun will come up tomorrow, the exploratory cystoscopy procedure and biopsy revealed another surprise blow – CANCER. Okay, so to cut short this chapter in my life, those dreaded weeks of chemotherapy, loss of weight, weakness, and test of tolerance didn't kill me. As fate would have it, and, as you all now know, I did not die. The treatment made me mentally stronger, and, although doing the act again was a mere hint of my former performances, my will to live was now greater than ever.

After a few weeks back at Casino Arizona, I forged my final "folly" in the Palm Springs Follies for the entire season. Taking voice lessons in Palm Springs in the hope that I could improve my pitch and range was able to turn an initial three note range into nine, just a little over an octave, but the quality was not much of an improvement. It took the help of an oxygen tank in the wings and an incredible amount of daily prescription drugs to get through the shows five days a week. In addition to the voice lessons, I started walking two miles a day every morning at dawn. Brad Cummings came to see me in the Follies and his booking in the show the following season was absolutely smashing. I was proud to have mentored the man, and I have been a part of his career throughout the many venues where he followed in my tracks.

Now back in Palm Springs, I received a phone call from Frank Yturria about doing a party, but I had to tell him of my condition. He didn't seem to mind that I was a little "under the weather" and suggested that we just have a small event at the El Dorado Country Club. I did my best, under the circumstances, and managed to put together a much smaller celebration for his 90th birthday. The "old bird" was an inspiration and a great example of "Damn the torpedoes, full speed ahead." It did me a lot of good to get up and get going. With a local five-piece combo, and comedian, David Gee, the event went off without a hitch. It was the best therapy I could have received!

I did a couple of fundraisers for the American Cancer Association and the National Arthritis Foundation, and I also did a show at the famous Ice House in Pasadena, California, for Rudy Moreno, a very funny comedian and show producer. Trying to hang on to my career, I realized I was kidding myself and that realization made my mental state more depressed again. So, at this point, I decided to leave the stage and focus on coaching others in the future. A few more dates here and there, another ventriloquist convention lecture, and, then, I offered Francisco's 12-minute act to other vents in an attempt to keep it alive. Almost anyone could perform it better than I could now, even without my many years of experience. The work had already been done; just like doing an impression already created by another impressionist.

That summer, I attended the Vent Haven conVENTion once more and performed with Francisco for the "last" time to a long standing ovation from about 500 fellow ventriloquists. Then, in a short ceremonial-style moment of acknowledgment narrated by Tom Ladshaw, I donated the raggedy,

Sammy King and Tom Ladshaw
at the "Farewell to Francisco"
Vent Haven ConVENTion performance

worn-out Francisco puppet to the Vent Haven museum where he took his place between the exhibits of Señor Wences and Paul Winchell. It was a fitting final resting place.

New York ventriloquist, Pete Michaels, added Francisco's 12-minute act to his own, and, within a couple of months, he posted it on youtube. Considering the amount of time and number of shows, Pete was performing the act very well. I thought it was good to have the act carry on, and I could not have done it better in my present condition. I started directing my time and attention to helping my student vents, who numbered more than 40 at the time. In addition to those student vents working in schools and libraries, there were many more in the ministries doing bible story parodies in their acts. To me, this seemed like a wonderful way of using the art to communicate, especially with children.

One of the best ventriloquists doing shows in the ministries was Yoly Pacheco, a beautiful Mexican-American woman from Phoenix, Arizona. We had met a couple of years before at the Vent Haven ConVEN-Tion in Kentucky. Yoly, her husband, Arnie, and daughter, Lindsay, were very spiritual and just being with them sharing quality time was most uplifting and inspiring to me. When I later played Casino Arizona again, they all came to see me, and I also visited with them at their home a couple of times. I encouraged Yoly to produce a Ventriloquist 101 course in Spanish since she was regularly playing huge venues while touring Central and South America and Mexico. She finally did make the video, and I did a short interview for her in Spanish.

The next year went by slower than any other I remembered in my stage career. There were zero performances. I stayed shut-up in a Palm Springs condominium building puppets with arthritis in my hands and trying in vain to play the guitar. When summer came around, I went to the 2013 ventriloquist conVENTion accompanied by my daughter, Kristi. It was her first trip to Vent Haven, and she took good care of me, staying close to organize and control my activities. After a few private one-on-one coaching sessions with attending vents, I gave a lecture and workshop entitled "Coach Yourself," a collection of my notes from past convention workshops on the finer points of performing an act on stage.

When the convention ended, Kristi and I drove to Pigeon Forge, Tennessee, to visit with David Hirschi, a comedy juggler that I knew from my *Comedy Cabaret* days at the Maxim Hotel in Vegas. David had been working in Branson for 20 years with a second company of *Country Tonite*, and he was the producer of Yakov Smirnoff's show for six years.

We talked about putting together a comedy show somewhere in Branson or finding a smaller venue somewhere in Tennessee. He was committed to a year's contract at The Smoky Mountain Opry in Pigeon Forge and had a vacant house in Branson where I could stay. I thought the idea might be good for me. Was it back to Branson again for me?

Branson Again
2013 – 2015

    Branson was in various stages of a downward spiral when I arrived. After meeting with local favorite, Jim Stafford, and learning that he was not opening his theater for another season, I met with Todd Oliver and Jim Barber, two great ventriloquist acts that had been enjoying great success in the Ozarks. Incidentally, whenever I asked anyone in Branson about the derivative of "Ozark," most folks said, "It's the name of the mountains." I would later inform them that it's actually from the French term, aux arc, which loosely translated means "of the woods." Jim Barber was in his final year at the Hamner Barber Theatre, and Todd Oliver was closing down his show at the Americana Theatre. It was a bad time to think of starting all over again in that town. Andy Williams had died of bladder cancer in 2012 (while I survived it), ending a successful run at his Moon River Theatre, and every other show in town seemed to be experiencing the worst attendance ever.

    The historic Owens Theatre in downtown Branson caught my eye because of its size. Rather than introduce myself and ask for comps, I bought tickets a couple of times to scope out the situation there. The show, called *Pure Comedy*, was an hour and a half with no intermission. Scripted by writers from *The Carol Burnett Show* and *Laugh In*, I thought maybe I could find a place in the show and slowly transition back to the stage. Since the theater only played four shows on two days a week, I thought I could handle the gig. I offered to showcase the act and joined the show. After a couple of months in *Pure Comedy*, a different show was added to the Owens Theatre's schedule. This new show, entitled *Vaudeville Laughternoon* was exactly what the name said – a mixture of acts: comedy, magic, juggling, quick-change, and, now, ventriloquism. Once again, Teddy was appearing as Buckaroo Buddy doing his own spot and Francisco's family-friendly version of the act. I felt as though I had come full circle to where it all started 65 years before, and I was finally back to performing on the stage and doing what I was born to do – ventriloquism!

Appendix A: The Coach

"...if you become a teacher, by your pupils you'll be taught."
-- Oscar Hammerstein

My coaching career actually began in 1989 with my return to Las Vegas from Paris, but it was actually more of an evolution than a sudden conversion. I met David Iannaci, a physical comic, in Reno some 20 years earlier during my engagement at Harrah's, and we became longtime friends and fellow performers. David and I exchanged ideas and experimented with different comedy styles, and, together, we sold the concept for a comedy show in Las Vegas and Laughlin, Nevada. In the end, we reaped the benefits of trying and, then, proving our hard work on stage. Between building props and writing different twists to old gags, I was coaching others and directing stage performances without even realizing the turn my career was taking.

Then, in 1990, I worked with Rick Michel, a Las Vegas impressionist, in a show called *Comedy Cabaret* at the Maxim Hotel in Vegas. Rick was doing a 12-minute act that included impressions of as many different celebrities as possible in that amount of time. He was also a great singer whose Frank Sinatra, Dean Martin, and Sammy Davis, Jr., impressions were absolutely amazing. Not all impressionists are necessarily good singers, but Rick, a protégé of the amazing Rich Little, considered himself a singer first. Just as with David Iannaci, Rick and I built props together, had extensive dialogue about comedy and stage presence, and even wrote a book on the subject called, *Live on Stage...Don't Die, Kill.* I think it's safe to say those sessions, and the ultimate results, gave me the tools I eventually used to become a director and coach.

After attending a couple of ventriloquist conventions, Mark Wade, Executive Director of the Vent Haven ConVENTions, asked me to lead a number of lectures and workshops. So, along with some help from Tom Ladshaw, a very knowledgeable ventriloquism historian, I wrote a couple of booklets to accompany my new role. My lectures and workshops at Vent Haven were very well-received, and I had more vents asking questions about my coaching than I expected. Suddenly, I was spending much more time online or on the phone and reviewing notes for class sessions. I found that, in order to continue coaching, it became a matter of pacing myself by limiting my days and hours of performing. But, the time spent was well worth the effort, and the reward was the same as teachers often receive from their pupils.

Some veteran ventriloquists at the 2013 Vent Haven ConVENTion:
(From left to right) Jerry Layne, Sammy King, Bob Isaacson,
Jimmy Nelson, Jim Teter, Jay Johnson

My newly-found joy in helping other vents learn from my many years of experience added a new aspect to my career. The more than 50 "students of the stage" with whom I have worked were not only ventriloquists, but also comedians and novelty acts. Coaching vents that normally work in other professions, but simply enjoy performing ventriloquism, has always been a joy for me. My students don't need the art as a means of making a living; they simply delight in walking on stage and entertaining, and yet their dedication to study, practice, and understanding is remarkable in that they were always open to learning from coaching sessions.

****

I kept most of my notes from coaching sessions in a file, and, as I was new to computers at the time, most of them were either handwritten or typed on a typewriter. I would make copies of sessions I prepared for my classes. Doing two shows a night, six nights a week, created a lot of time to write what I learned from my thousands of trips to the stage. More than 20 years later, here are just a few of those notes:

CHARACTER

Commitment to character cannot be over emphasized. There are two kinds of acting – good and bad. Good acting is being present and RE-ACTING. Bad acting is coming from nowhere and trying to go somewhere. Stay present, pay attention, BE your character and simply BECOME. Not knowing your script will certainly inhibit your character. KNOW YOUR LINES. The more prepared you are, the less chance of failure. Be authentic. Any audience can sniff out a fraud or someone not into the character. You might think that your character is just being yourself, but who you are is not the same as who you must be for your audience. Talent is a gift to be shared with others. A waste of talent is the saddest thing I know. Imagination gives you wings. When you get an idea, stay with it and work it until it's done, and done right.

DERAILMENTS

During every beat of every performance, there is a DERAILMENT lurking. The possibility of getting sidetracked by some unexpected interruption is always present. It can be as simple as the sound of someone in the audience coughing, a telephone ringing, microphone feedback, prop malfunction...the list is endless. Some of them should be addressed and some ignored. Making that decision is risky. Do you leave the script and venture into the unknown? Is the audience even aware of the potential sidetrack? Losing your place or going blank on stage is, to say the least, unsettling. On the other hand, a clever improv may get the audience on your side; but, it is risky.

THE ROOM

One of the most important considerations when performing is determining the nature of the room. The same type room will vary in feeling from one location to another. Don't confuse the room with the audience. They are two very different things. The room is the audience's geographical area that determines where you will be sending your energy. A half-empty room must not be played the same as when it is a "packed house." Also, when

doing a sound check before a show, know it will not be the same once the room is filled with sound-soaking bodies.

TIMING

It's been said that timing is everything. It's not, but it is way ahead of whatever is in second place. I don't think timing can be taught. But, if you learn to pay attention and do enough shows, you will find that comedic timing is much like music – it has a tempo. A well-rehearsed script will certainly improve your timing, even if it's not natural to you. Learning to play an instrument doesn't make you a player, but one can certainly improve with enough practice. Timing is not something you can clock, but it will serve you well to tune into your audience. Playing a room that seats 2,000 will require considerations in the amount of time it takes the performer to get a reaction. I learned from experience how different and difficult it can be to wait for a reaction.

There were many other notes on various subjects that I would later put in two books, *Coach Yourself* and *Live on Stage*. In addition to writing more new material for Francisco's act, I decided to redeem my Branson blunder by writing a family-friendly script. (See Appendix D)

I have included comments from four different vents who have applied my coaching observations and notes to give a perspective from the sessions they received. Levi Attias is a lawyer in Gibraltar. Jimmy Vee is a marketing executive in Orlando, Florida. Mark Hellerstein is a retired oil company CEO in Denver, Colorado, and Bob Baker is a gastroenterologist in New York.

****

<u>LEVI J. ATTIAS</u>

It is said that when the student is ready, the teacher will appear. Drawn as I am to the performing arts in many of its guises, some years back I took a stab at ventriloquism. Sporadically, I took face to face private lessons with ventriloquists and I avidly read as many books as possible on the subject. Following as if by rote, I dabbled and practiced exercises, as best I could, contained in the wealth of DVD's I acquired. Although I am quite self-motivated, I needed to generate enough motivation for two; Lola the Monkey (my first dummy) and myself. That was a tall order! I believe I was 'led to' Sammy King. One evening, as I was scouring the internet for ventriloquist scripts, I saw a recording of Sammy at (I believe) Vent Haven 2012. Within minutes of reading about Sammy, I emailed him to inquire on the viability of distant coaching. I reside in Gibraltar. Some three hours later, Sammy and I were in email contact. We realized we shared a number of personal attributes including our bilingualism (English and Spanish). Our rapport was deep and immediate.

Deep-rooted affinity between coach and student is elementary for successful coaching, especially one conducted across the oceans. Sammy became my ventriloquism coach and mentor. I worked on the exercises he personalized for me, (intonations, labials, manipulation, script, you name it) over a period of a fortnight or so. I would then record my restructured act and send Sammy a recording via email taking on board his observations and suggestions. Some days later, we would chat on the phone for a solid hour during which Sammy would review and critique my developing skills. We would pore over the script, delve into manipulation, work on lip control and anything else that cropped up. Over many months, Sammy became my flesh and blood link to the engrossing world of ventriloquism. His coaching, at a vast geographic distance, proved immensely successful

111

and stunningly productive; within a few months, I was flapping my wings (or straight-jacketing my lips) as a novice ventriloquist in the Spanish and English languages. Sammy encouraged, goaded and inspired me with four seminal C's: comments, critique, compliments and companionship. I am humbled and honored to call him my "big C" – my Coach!

****

JIMMY VEE

I have been interested in ventriloquism for over thirty years and performing for just over twenty. It is through ventriloquism that many of the greatest things in my life have transpired, and I believe that it has colored nearly every part of my life and contributed greatly to who I am today.

I put myself through college doing ventriloquism shows. I met some of my oldest friends because of ventriloquism. I proposed to my wife using ventriloquism. Ventriloquism helped get me through the financial difficulty of being a new father and starting a business, and ventriloquism has connected me to some of the most amazing people I've ever known – not to mention the joy and laughter it's allowed me to share with those people.

One of the first ventriloquist performances I can remember that really blew me away was Sammy King's bit on the HBO *Dummies* special from 1978. I actually didn't see it live. I saw it by chance. I was at a friend's house, and he mentioned the show and played a tape of it for me. I remember that day because that performance made a huge impact on me. It opened my eyes to how powerful and innovative ventriloquism can be.

When it came to ventriloquism, I wanted to be as good as Sammy King. I wanted to be that natural, that polished, that creative, that funny, that edgy, and that skilled…. I wanted to be a showman. I wanted to be everything that Sammy is. That show has always been my inspiration. In the last few years, I had really wanted to expand my ventriloquism and performance from kid and family shows to comedy clubs and eventually create a one-man theater show.

While building my advertising and marketing agency, I learned that finding mentors was a huge leverage point that allowed me to move forward faster in nearly any endeavor I wanted to undertake. I figured ventriloquism would be no different, so I set out to find a ventriloquism mentor – a task I did not think would be simple.

After a bit of searching and asking around, I had heard that Sammy King was acting as a coach to a select group of ventriloquists. I couldn't believe it. If I were to hand-select a single ventriloquist who had impacted my ventriloquism journey, it would be Sammy. I jumped at the chance to have him mentor me.

I reached out to Sammy about coaching me, and he asked that I send over a video of me performing my ventriloquism routine. I told him that I didn't have a routine yet for the type of ventriloquism show I wanted to create. I was afraid I wouldn't catch Sammy's interest and that he would not want to coach me. Not being one to be deterred, I sent him a video of me doing some ad-lib vent work and hoped for the best. To my delight, Sammy accepted. He saw a spark in me that he liked, and he became my coach, my mentor, and now I am honored to say, my friend.

Being coached by Sammy has been more than I could have ever imagined it would be. I learned so much so fast. Sammy's wisdom is only overshadowed by his willingness to share. At the time I connected with Sammy, he was recovering from some major health issues and had difficulty talking, but that didn't stop Sammy. He was dedicated to my success, and I was a dedicated student. I was a sponge and wanted to soak up whatever knowledge I could. I quickly realized that Sammy and I were kindred spirits. We spent much time working together remotely and in person. Throughout that time, I learned so much, grew tremendously as a vent and a performer and as a person.

Sammy has taught me many things: how to confidently enter a stage, how to project my personality to an audience, how to begin my show performance for maximum impact, how to win over a crowd with a smile, how to create strong character with movement, how to introduce myself and my partner (more importantly, what not to do), how to punch up material to get more laughs, how to pause, when to keep quiet, how to slow down, how to end an act, how to critically analyze my own practice and performances, with and without sound, and how to never give up, just to name a few. All of these lessons made me a better ventriloquist and performer and boosted my confidence.

I took that confidence and moved forward with Sammy helping me put together a comedy routine for clubs, which I performed at the IMPROV, as well as accomplishing many other goals I had set for myself as a ventriloquist. We're still working together today, and I have much to learn and more I want to accomplish. The good news is that Sammy has a lot more to teach and share.

I went to Sammy to find a ventriloquism coach, but what I got was much, much more. What I got was a mentor in life and a friend for eternity.

****

BOB BAKER

The first time I saw Sammy King live, he took himself apart. At the 2012 Vent Haven ConVENTion, Sammy opened his lecture with a video of himself performing with Francisco on an HBO ventriloquism special. He asked the assembled vents to rate the performance. Most thought it was great; I know I did. Wrong.

Sammy proceeded to dissect his own performance, pointing out flaws, poor stagecraft, bad timing, etc. Moment by moment, in excruciating detail, he critiqued himself mercilessly. When I was done being stunned by this self-deconstruction, I thought to myself, "This is a guy who really, really knows showmanship, and I want him to teach me."

I approached Sammy afterward with a bit of trepidation. After all, he's a legendary figure among ventriloquists. The man himself, though, was kind, garrulous and approachable, and I knew – at age 61 – that I'd found my mentor.

Since then, Sammy has applied the same keen showbiz eye to my own performances, and I believe my performing skills have improved greatly. As important, he has helped me learn to watch videos of my own performances (so painful!) and analyze them as he did his own.

Once, during one of our phone conferences, I told Sammy that I was going to watch the semi-finals of *America's Got Talent* live. He said, "When you're there, picture yourself on that stage." It had never even occurred to me to consider auditioning for *America's Got Talent*, but Sammy had planted the seed. The next season I sent in a tape and was chosen to audition for the producers and, then, the "celebrity judges."

My coach and mentor helped me prepare. *America's Got Talent* gives you only 90 seconds to show your stuff, so Sammy helped me make sure that every second counted. He helped me edit lines, cut out unnecessary words, and perfect the timing of the jokes. He watched video after video, helping me hone my performance.

The audition went fabulously well. The audience was laughing so hard, I had to keep stopping to let the laughter die down. I finished with chants of "Vegas! Vegas!" raining down on me from the audience of 1500 people. It was a great feeling.

Should you look up my audition on *YouTube*, though, you'll see something very different. Because one of the judges, Howard Stern, is my patient, the executive producer told me ahead of time that no matter how well I did, he could not allow me to advance in the competition. So *America's Got Talent* chopped up my performance and actually changed two of the judges' votes to portray the result they wanted.

No matter. It was a great experience. Hell, I got to do ventriloquism on TV for 11 million people! But, it wouldn't have happened if it weren't for Sammy King. He gave me the inspiration, the skills, and the courage to reach higher than I thought possible. And isn't that what a mentor does?

P.S. Now Sammy is coaching me in performing Francisco, and I am both humbled and honored that he would allow me to carry on this great act.

****

MARK HELLERSTEIN

In 1997, I was attending a breakfast at the Las Vegas Vent Convention and happened to sit at a table with Sammy King. Little did I know that this moment would have a major impact on my life. I am sure Sammy does not remember that breakfast. But I do. He mentioned that he was starting to mentor/coach a few acts. I thought to myself that this could be an opportunity of a lifetime…to be coached by one of the greats. I was 45 years old at the time and had been passionate about vent from the moment I read Paul Winchell's book at the age of 10. I knew that I had good technical skills, but in my heart of hearts, I also knew that I needed more. Sammy could be the one to help me reach that next level.

I sent a video of several performances to Sammy and approximately three months later, the phone rang. "This is Sammy King. I reviewed your video. You don't have an act. It is merely a string of jokes. I can help you." And, so began an amazing journey. Over the next 18 years, my level of performance has soared. I now have approximately three hours of rock solid material that has been polished and honed under Sammy's amazing eye. And, most importantly, I have a true and lifelong friend in Sammy. Describing the journey and coaching process is not easy. Therefore, rather than documenting a chronology of events, I will try to describe the most important lessons that I learned along the way, together with the process. Working with a Coach

I believe working with any coach requires certain elements to be successful:

• I had seen Sammy's act a number of times and truly admired his work. I had complete confidence in his knowledge and competence. I also knew from his initial phone call that he is direct and sometimes brutally honest.
• I was at a point in my life where all I wanted to do was improve. I was not going to let my ego fight his advice. I did everything he told me to do, without questioning its validity.
• I listened carefully and took notes of every comment/instruction and practiced diligently to implement the changes.

Building an Act

Sammy and I have worked on a number of different acts: Professor Penwell, Pansy the baby chimpanzee, Frankenstein, Jack and the Bean-stalk (a ventriloquial marionette show), DoReMe, J.P. Morgan, Willie Worm the Bookworm, Torrance N. Tabor, Buckaroo Buddy, and a Sammy King Francisco tribute. Sammy's involvement has ranged from writing the entire act initially to reviewing my writing with minor changes. Each act generally ranges from 5-15 minutes and has a clear beginning, middle, and end. The comedy and writing is character-based.

Our initial agreement was for Sammy to create an adult act for me and to coach me on performing it. He had seen my early videos and took elements from my work as well as elements from my business background and wrote an act. We met for dinner at the Aladdin Hotel in Las Vegas (Sammy was performing in the *Country Tonite* production show). Sammy pulled out drawings of his concept: I would walk onto the stage with a suitcase, flip it open into a stand with a drawing board (Axtell), draw a picture of the Professor which comes to life, flip the board down and the Professor is there in person, have the comedy routine, include a technique song that I previously did in the middle (Sammy to add music), end with a Houdini-like escape where the Professor is handcuffed, blindfolded, and folded back into the suitcase, and have a surprise ending with a saw blade (and my saw impression) sawing out the Professor. WOW! AN ACT!

Of course, I had to figure out how to make a case that does all this. After a number of false starts, I made a prototype and found someone who works in aluminum that could turn it into reality. After 18 years, the structure of the act is unchanged: a magical beginning, comedy, technical song, and magical ending. And, with many shows under my belt, the dialogue evolved and has probably changed by 90%. The Professor also changed dramatically. He originally was a used Selberg figure (Selberg's 3rd figure ever made), which only had a poorly working mouth and was very heavy. I sent him back to Selberg to add the marvelous Selberg mechanics; reshape the head, hollow it out, and repaint him...now a masterpiece.

Endearing Character

"Commitment to character." Sammy says it over and over. I believe these were the words Edgar Bergen spoke to Sammy after complimenting him on his act. Sammy describes his act as an international act. This means that the humor is character-based as opposed to standard jokes. It's not to say there aren't funny lines, but rather the lines are coming from somewhere. It is not a string of jokes. In a workshop that I teach, I use a variety of video clips of the greatest vents' greatest moments. Of the vents in the Golden age of the 1930s-1950s, kids laugh the most at Señor Wences. His humor is ageless as it is solely character-based. The material of other vents of that era is not as funny today as "joke-type" humor changes with time.

My most endearing and funniest puppet is Pansy, a baby chimpanzee. And, she does not say a word. Her humor is quite physical and visual. She is very lovable. The act evolved over time. Sammy had made the "Pansy" puppet for someone else, but it didn't work out, so he sold her to me. He gave me some rough ideas and a start. The rest was developing specific bits that evolved to be very funny...only because of her endearing character.

Surprisingly, the most "character" comments by Sammy were not about my puppet's character, but rather about my character. It is really my character that helps give stature to the act and bring out the comedy of the puppet. Several years ago, Sammy gave a lecture on how an act evolves and showed video clips of his act from about 1970 on *The Ed Sullivan Show*, continuously in time to the present. What was so amazing was that Francisco's personality changed little over that time. But, the "Sammy" character changed dramatically. Initially, "Sammy" laughed nervously at Francisco's lines. That laugh totally disappeared and was replaced by a more serious "Sammy" that reacted to Francisco's lines and antics. THAT is what made Francisco so funny. I have heard that the straight man to yesteryear's comedy teams always made more money than the comic partner, as the key to getting the big laughs was the straight man's personality and reactions.

One of my signature acts is my Frankenstein act. Before I met Sammy, I had a Frankenstein adventure (without puppets) that ended with a four-minute ventriloquial recreation of the Frankenstein experiment. Sammy thought the ending could be a complete 12-minute act. We collaborated and created a very unique act. There are actually five characters in the act (Dr. Frankenstein, narrator, Baltimore/Frankenstein and a talking skull). What Sammy thought was critical was for Dr. Frankenstein (played by me) to be over the top while the narrator (also me, but with glasses off) to be very subdued and mild. Sammy felt the contrast and change in "volume" would make the Dr. Frankenstein character much bigger and better…and Sammy was right (as usual).

Whenever I am in the early stages of learning a new act, Sammy's comments always focus on adding more reaction from the "Mark" character. This is difficult to learn and requires much practice. For me, it usually comes later in my learning as the material has to be second nature at that stage of development.

Splitting

Over the years, I found that I liked some vents' work much better than others even though they all had good technique and characters. The difference is "splitting," having both the ventriloquist and puppet characters alive at the same time and acting appropriately to the moment. Paul

Winchell first coined this term in his teaching DVD. Sammy and Winchell are, by far, better at splitting than any other vents. And, it raises the believability of the characters to a much greater height. Sammy focused on this very early in his lessons with me. When watching one of my video performances, Sammy would cover half of the screen showing just the puppet and, then, the other half showing just me. We watched to make sure that both characters were alive throughout the performance. Unfortunately, splitting is incredibly difficult to actually do. Sammy had me work on muscle memory by having me memorize the physical movements for me and the puppet separately (and slowly) and getting them into muscle memory and, then, combining them. It is definitely well worth the effort as it raised the level of performance tremendously.

Comedy

Sammy constantly works on making my act funnier. He has a great sense of humor. Here are some of the things he does:

- He looks for opportunities to have a running gag. Three is the magic number and they always start off small (subtle) with the third one being big.
- He always looks to make a line simpler.
- He looks to change the phrasing or emphasis to make it funnier.
- He never stops making the changes (see discussion of 100 X 100).

Staging, Music, and Props

Sammy loves good staging, music, and props, and he has a masterful eye. He views all props as prototypes just waiting to be improved upon. He also focuses on transitions to make them seamless. I talked about the great prop for Professor Penwell, which is not only the structure of an act, but it is a way to have the Professor seamlessly make his appearance and then disappear at the end of the act. In Frankenstein, I not only go in and out of costume seamlessly, but the puppets and props appear and disappear almost without the audience realizing it. Sammy is also a very good artist and loves making props and puppets of different kinds. He has made Pansy, Buckaroo Buddy, my hypodermic needle and props for DoReMe. He has arranged for music and lyrics as well.

119

However, Sammy's most amazing feat was with my marionette program of Jack and the Beanstalk. I wanted to create an act that would appeal to a younger audience and thought storytelling via a marionette show using ventriloquism would work great. I had never worked with marionettes and was able to find a puppet-maker that made good puppet characters for me. Unfortunately, I couldn't find a stage, so I made one myself. I also "cut and pasted" some music together. Sammy attended my second performance ever and didn't like the music and backdrops and quickly had them redone by professionals. He also didn't like the way one could see the puppets entering and exiting the stage and gave me some ideas on how to make it better. I had a person who works in aluminum make a new type of frame with fabric covering. I started using it, but the kids in the back could not see the puppets, so I had to have the stage re-made on a "stilt" concept. This third stage worked fairly well...but it was not enough. About one to two years later, Sammy had a brainstorm – if we could add electric curtains, built-in music, floodlights, spot lights, black light, strobe light, and fogger, it would take the act to a whole other level. Sammy then took it upon himself to make it happen. He brought the stage to my house via a truck. It did all of those things. Unfortunately, it was very bulky and clumsy and never got out of my garage. BUT, it was a big step and a great prototype. Sammy knew the set designer for a local theater and brought him to my house. After much discussing and measuring, he came up with an amazing stage that folds up and fits in my SUV and does everything Sammy dreamed. He first made a steel prototype and then the aluminum stage (stage number 6). Now, I had to learn to do a marionette show with ventriloquism while managing scenery, music, lighting, fogger and curtains. Sammy loved it as I am visible to the audience. While the kids see the story of Jack and the Beanstalk, the parents enjoy watching me as a one-man band. It is truly a masterpiece and a great act. Thanks to Sammy for always trying to improve and rethink what is being done.

Derailments

Sammy has never had a perfect show after 25,000 performances. There is always a derailment of some kind: a "brain fart," a cough or sneeze in the audience, a heckler, someone arriving late or leaving early. In his sessions, Sammy helps prepare his students for these mishaps. He tries to keep you "in the moment" and able to respond, or not respond, as appropriate or cover while forgetting a missed line.

During sessions with Sammy, he generally reviews a live or video performance and, then, proceeds to make corrections. In the early stages of an act, my notes can easily run 5-10 pages. His changes vary and may include:

- Eliminating the negatives. In my case, I had a habit of crinkling my forehead during a performance. He also didn't like my glasses as they could reflect light into someone's eyes.
- Changing the wording.
- Changing the physical action.
- Changing the way something is said or in the action/reaction.

100 X 100

Sammy says that an act is not ready until it has been practiced 100 times and performed 100 times. The practice is necessary to polish and perfect the material and to make it second nature, so that you can think about other things (than your lines) during the performance. But you can't create the pressure and timing of a live audience. Sammy suggests practicing to a video camera rather than to a mirror for two reasons. With a mirror, the ventriloquist is focusing on looking in that spot rather than on "splitting." It also allows the vent to start over when there is a mistake. The video camera simulates a live audience and creates a similar pressure. The vent must learn to cover for mistakes and perform under pressure. It also allows the vent to view the performance as an outsider does.

But, there is nothing as good as "time on the boards," i.e., live performances. Here the vent learns to master the timing and also tries different ways of doing things to see what works best. The act evolves during this process through the feedback of a live audience. As a comedian, you will find that a show for one audience gets great laughs while another show may not. Hopefully, you can increase the positive percentage significantly. But, there will always be times the audience is not laughing as expected. This used to discourage me; I would get "flop sweat" and proceed to speed up my tempo. Sammy taught me that some audiences aren't big laughers (usually it takes several instigators in the audience to get them going), but are still enjoying the show very much. This advice gave me the confidence to enjoy every show and do my best. I, personally, have found the 100 X 100 rule of thumb is pretty accurate.

Conclusion

Nowhere have I talked about ventriloquism, i.e., talking without moving the lips. Sammy does not teach these basics. Instead, he teaches comedy and show business. These are the lessons that are usually glossed over in most books on vent.

As a youngster, my dream was to be a professional vent performing on TV or in Las Vegas. Instead, I led a "normal" life and had a successful business career. Fortunately, I was able to retire at a relatively young age, so that I could follow my passion for ventriloquism. However, I was at a stage in life that I didn't want to travel to pursue my dreams. Therefore, I decided to follow my passion in Colorado where I determined the market was focused primarily on kids. Sammy made it clear to me that what is important is not the prestige or size of the venue, but rather the quality of the performance. I am so grateful to him, as the quality of my programs has advanced way beyond my wildest imagination, and I continue to enjoy every minute. All thanks to a chance breakfast at the Vent Convention with Sammy King.

Appendix B: Love and Family in Ventriloquism

I can't help but want to say a few words about love and the women in my life throughout my career. It is curious to me that a ventriloquist has a love for his art that may, or may not, be understood by others. I believe it takes a very special kind of woman to share her life with a performer. Not all, but most of the ventriloquists I know have had more than one spouse or partner. I suppose there is a certain amount of jealousy involved, but not the kind that is usually associated with marriage. I think it's more about the amount of time and commitment to the art of ventriloquism that is the problem. As with every art form, performance and practice take up a lot of hours in each day. To be great at anything requires time and dedication. As ventriloquists, we get a kick out of what we create with our love of entertaining. What could be more gratifying than to make someone "forget their troubles and just get happy," as the song goes? There is a notion that playing with puppets is childish, but giving "life" to a character is serious business.

I married four beautiful women. I don't know if that is anything to brag about, but it is a fact. A vent is well-served to have an additional partner other than the ones found in figures, puppets, dummies, or whatever you wish to call those characters embodied in a lifeless prop. Sharing a life with someone is not only natural, it is easier. Helping one another, sharing experiences, and exchanging ideas are all wonderful examples of what it means to go through life with someone. Loneliness always knows what to expect; a partnership is full of discoveries. I am grateful for all the women who have helped me through my journey as a performing artist, including my daughters. I don't know if I could have done it without them, but it has been great fun doing it with them.

#1 Judy Jacobs – The Original Mrs. King

Sammy King and I met in 1962 when his uncle, Manuel King, was negotiating the sale of two of my mother's (Dolly Jacobs) elephants during the Texas Shrine Circus dates. We met, dated, and married too soon in a civil ceremony at the Fort Worth, Texas, courthouse. After the circus tour was over, we lived for a couple of months in Houston, where I worked with Sammy in some children's shows as a magician's assistant. Then, we lived in a trailer in Gainesville, Texas, on my mother's property. Sammy was a year and a half younger than I, but he was talented and ambitious.

I felt he needed to find his way without me, and we divorced within the year. We remain loving friends.

Judy Jacobs King Kaye

#2 Tita Toro – Second Chance

I was nineteen when I met Sammy. He had come to see *A Funny Thing Happened on the Way to the Forum* in which I was performing. There he was at the stage door waiting to meet me. He wanted me to perform in a show that he was producing, *Laugh Laugh Laugh*, which I did. That started a wonderful relationship. Later, after we were married, we toured with the USO that first year. I saw parts of the world you only dream about and experienced so many different things. It was always such a thrill to be performing on the same stage and in the same show with Sammy. A year later, we went back overseas, and, this time, besides doing his amazing act, he also accompanied me on flamenco guitar while I danced.

Sammy was very much a perfectionist and was constantly working on improving his act as well as improving Francisco. He went through many parrots while we were together. His audiences truly loved him. We had five years together, and they were always filled with fun and excitement.

He gave me an amazingly talented daughter, who gave us an amazing granddaughter, so I always get to have a part of him. We parted in 1971. We see each other often and will always be close.

Tita Toro King Piazza Jackson

#3 Barbara Lauren – "Miss Broadway"

My life with a ventriloquist was never dull! I met my first husband, Sammy King, when I was 21 years old. Friends introduced us, and then we were performing in a show together at The Carillon Hotel in Miami. The day before we met, I saw him on *The Ed Sullivan Show*. I was a goner.... Love at first laugh. We married two months after we met. Then, the fun really began. I followed Sammy and his trusted puppet, Francisco, wherever the show bookings were. He loved to perform – all of him loved to perform. I say "all" because I realized I was living with many different Sammy's, and I don't mean his dummies. He had definite different personalities, so distinctly different from each other that I had names for each one. Keep in mind this was NOT schizophrenia; it was just different "moods" he possessed. He was:

Eddie – tough and not so kind

Freddie – the life of the party and so very funny

Ronald – the hopeless romantic

Donald – the world traveler and dreamer

…and *Sammy*, who equaled all of the above

As a 21-year-old madly in love, I mastered treating and loving all of them equally. I learned so much about show business from Sammy; mostly how to treat people kindly from the producers to the backstage help. Whenever you mention Sammy King's name in the business, it's greeted with the utmost respect. I was pretty smart to fall in love at first laugh…

Barbara Lorrie Firkser Lauren King Hirsch Ryan

#4 Leigh Cassidy – A Dancer's Dancer

I've always hated clowns and ventriloquists. That is, until the fall of 1974, when I met Sammy King. We were working in a Barry Ashton production at the Americana Hotel in Miami Beach. Our wardrobe mistress came into our dressing room one night, raving about the closing act. We dancers had never really even seen the act, as our rehearsals for the show had been separate in Los Angeles, prior to being sent to Florida.

All we knew about Sammy King's act was "100 dollars, are you out of your mind?" which was our cue to get downstairs and set up for the finale. My curiosity got the best of me, as Norah, from wardrobe, would watch the act every night and return to us repeating the lines. I remember telling her I didn't like ventriloquists…creepy, but she insisted I go with her. Reluctantly, I finally went to see for myself. In a matter of 12 minutes, my mind was completely changed from annoyed beyond words at having been talked into something I didn't really want to do, to complete curiosity of this art form I had always dismissed.

Sammy's act has changed considerably over all these years, but the one thing that has never changed is his love for his work. I've never known anyone who loves to work as much as this man. If, and when, he ever took a vacation; sure enough about 5pm, wherever he happened to be, his body would go into "auto pilot," and he'd start getting nervous, in anticipation of a show. "Relax Sammy. Enjoy your time off," we would tell him. He didn't. He would have rather been on stage.

Another bit of his personality that I always found so interesting; this is a man who, after a performance, finds the nearest kitchen exit, back door escape, or service elevator to remove himself as quickly as possible from a showroom. Sammy has always been shy about running into audience members after a show and hearing praise from his fans. It has never been part of his personality to thrive, or depend, on such things. Then, one day, show producers came up with the bright idea of "meet and greet," which about destroyed him. He couldn't get out of those lines fast enough!

Sammy King is one of a kind. We have all been blessed knowing him for all these years and privileged to enjoy his work.

Leigh Cassidy King

Elizabeth Bendgen – My Guardian Angel

I first met Sammy while I was working at the Palm Springs Follies as a dresser. One of my duties was to escort some of the acts, and stars, to and from their dressing room to the stage, wait there off stage behind the curtain while they performed their act, and then escort them back to their dressing room. It wasn't that they were easily confused or could get lost, the theater was just very old and built as a movie house – not for shows. So, it was easy to get turned around, and the producer/director thought it best that an escort guide the way for safety reasons.

I had never heard of Sammy King before, let alone seen his act. From the very first time I heard him (I was backstage and couldn't see him), he made me laugh and for every show after that, too. When I finally did get to see him on stage, he certainly did not disappoint. I loved it. We got to know each other a little better, and he promised to make me laugh every day. Except for when he was in a coma in the hospital, he's kept his promise.

The thing that surprised me the most about Sammy is how nervous he is before each and every show. For two whole seasons in the Palm Springs Follies, I was assigned to escort him from the dressing room to his pre-set position in the wings prior to his stage entrances. He was sweating, pacing, and mumbling, "I can't do this...is it too late to back out now?" I would bring him tissues to dry his face and a small battery fan to cool him, but nothing would work. The last thing he did before his entrance was check his fly for the third time. After more than nine years, that never changed, but, as soon as he takes his first step on stage, all that goes away, and he is in total control. When he exits, he is the first to question what he was so nervous about...go figure!

Elizabeth Ann Bendgen

Alicia King Dunfee, Daughter

I was lucky. I didn't know any different. I spent the majority of my life with Mom, but every summer with Dad. This was my "normal," which I would guess is different for most children of divorce. I got to see the world. By the time I was 15, I had spent three summers touring Europe, the Bahamas, and nearly every backstage dressing room from Las Vegas to Miami. The school year was spent studying various types of dance, singing, and musical theatre; summers were about how to put it all to good use.

Dad offered me my first professional contract. He tried to teach me how to speak Spanish. (I failed miserably.) He tried to teach me how to play the guitar. (Nope.) And, when the teen years hit, I gave my father a run for his money as every good daughter should. We grew apart. We grew back together – stronger than imaginable. I went on to have a successful stage career of my own. And, every time I was "on the boards," I felt my dad. The best gift he gave me was comedic timing. It is still debatable as to whether that can be taught, but it's something we thrive on discussing. Together, we have a mutual understanding for performance, and I think we relish in each other's notes – although Dad says he prefers kosher pickles...

All of this is important to me. All of these things make me who I am, and it barely scratches the surface as far as what this parent gave his daughter. But, my greatest lesson from my father was learned this past year. Now that his oldest daughter is raising her own daughter, I can reflect on the many different phases of my Dad's life. Most were hugely successful. Some were a struggle. But, the constant was this: Be happy. Do what you love. To give even 20 minutes of your life bringing joy to others will make you richer than any paycheck you may receive. Do your best. Love with all of your heart.

Alicia King Dunfee

Kristi-Ann King, Daughter

My father always said I was "Born in a Trunk." I had the amazing opportunity of starting my worldly travels as an infant. Dad was working at the Crazy Horse in Paris, so that was home for the first five years of my life. We then landed in the Bahamas, where I attended Kindergarten, spent evenings backstage in the dressing room, and occasionally visited the local beach club, where Dad and I once danced to "Tiny Winy, Tiny Boom Boom." I then shared the stage with Dad in Laughlin, where I filled in as Teddy. The wardrobe belonged to one of his many dwarfs, and was too small for me even at age nine. I was so nervous the whole time, but I knew Dad wouldn't let me fail. I jumped off the stool at the end of the act, walked off stage, and stood there in the wings listening to the great applause he got for singing "Old McDonald." I was so proud of him.

I remember spending numerous years at the Aladdin Hotel and Casino in Las Vegas, where Dad lived in the Elvis Presley Honeymoon Suite. I would go down nightly with him to watch the show, *Country Tonite*, and especially to watch his act. I knew every single line of it and would lip-sync it in the audience, looking around waiting for everyone to respond and start laughing. I also had the pleasure of working in *Showstoppers Live*, both in Arizona and Oklahoma with Dad.

Sharing the stage and seeing how everyone loved him was the best. We also had many road trips together where I accompanied him as a Mariachi. That was always fun. My Dad gave me a dummy, Howdy Doody, when I was young. I always tried to do ventriloquism and imitate Dad for my friends. I have always looked up to Dad and his work ethic. He would live and die on stage if he could. My Dad's philosophy is: Worry only about today, honor your parents, and always do the right thing. I will never stop being proud of my father. After all, he is The King!

Kristi-Ann King

Appendix C: The Interview

(In his dressing room backstage at the Plaza Theatre in Palm Springs, a relaxed Sammy King is in-between shows. There is a wardrobe rack in one corner, a dressing table with a mirror surrounded by lights, a guitar case, and a bird cage on a stand covered by a Mexican serape. There's a picture of his daughters taped on the mirror. He is drinking water from a paper cup and dressed in shorts, a tee shirt, and sandals.)

Writer: This is your return engagement to "The Palm Springs Follies." You were a big hit the last time you were here for the 10th season. As a performer, are you more comfortable in this show, having performed here before?

Sammy: Well, of course. It generally takes me about two weeks to find the correct feel for any room, even here in a theater where everyone is facing the stage. I'm used to working mostly cabarets where tables take up a lot of space, there's nightclub noise, and cocktail waitresses are walking around taking drink orders and serving. This is a great venue for an act like mine.

Writer: What about the audiences; are they the same for you or is it different working to an older crowd?

Sammy: That's a good question. I think that my act transcends age; it's in classic form. I'm older myself now, so the audiences here at the Follies accept me and get into what I'm doing almost immediately. When I was a young man in my 20s and 30s, older people sometimes looked at me like a threat, especially during my long hair and beard era. And, there were a lot of places that simply wouldn't book me. Basically, I find audiences are the same all over the world; they're just people. I'm used to performing to a variety of ages and cultures.

Writer: There are a great number of celebrities that live in the Palm Springs area, and many of them come to see the Follies. Does it make a difference in your performance knowing they are in the audience? Do you still get butterflies in your stomach or are you confident?

Sammy: Generally, the cast isn't told who is in the audience at the Follies, and I like it that way. But, I still get a rush of adrenaline before every show, anyway. It's that "fear of failure" possibility.

Writer: Even after all these years of doing it? Is it worse sometimes than others?

Sammy: On opening night in any room, there is extra pressure because

I haven't experienced what it is like with an audience. I can get a sense of what the sound and lights are going to be like in rehearsal. But, even a sound check won't be the same once the house is filled with bodies.

Writer: What was it like on opening night at the Follies this year?

Sammy: Well, I believe that talent is God-given. And, there is a responsibility that goes along with it and that is to do the best I can every time I walk out on stage. When we opened here this season, I had just come off a long run at the Sahara in Vegas with Charo's show, so the act was polished. But, I was down with an allergy, so the thought of not being able to physically do ventriloquism because of a very sore throat made things very intense.

Writer: Can you elaborate on that? What were you feeling right up to the time you stepped out on stage?

Sammy: My life flashed before me; I mean my life on stage – not the shows that ended in "bravos," but all the shows when something went wrong, and I was wondering if this was going to be the next time. I had walked out on stage more than 20,000 times since I was 12 years old, and, now, 50 years later, I was thinking of those. The worst thing that can happen to a ventriloquist is an attack of laryngitis or something akin to it. So, I'm in the wings just before going on stage, and my throat is raw and covered with nodes, and all the worst memories of my career are all I can think about. Then, as I'm checking my fly to be sure it's zipped up – that's the last thing I do before every entrance – I hear my introduction, I take my first step toward the microphone, and the fear is gone, once again.

Writer: Have you been a ventriloquist all your life?

Sammy: (pause) Not yet.

Writer: How did you discover you could do ventriloquism? Did you see someone on television or...

Sammy: I heard a distant voice. There wasn't any television in my hometown when I first started. It's too long a story to tell right now...

Writer: Tell me about your guitar.

Sammy: It's a signed 1969 Manuel Contreras flamenco guitar.

Writer: No, I mean about playing. It sounds like you've spent some time on the instrument.

Sammy: Well, I don't consider myself a musician. I have too much respect for those who are gifted with the art, but I've been playing since I was a kid.

Writer: What are some of the things you play or listen to?

Sammy: I play classical guitar music that I've memorized over the years. I probably know about 30 pieces by heart, but, then, so what? I mostly listen to jazz, but I really like everything, except bagpipes.

Writer: It's clever, the way you use the guitar in the act.

Sammy: That's part of the evolution of the act, not anything I created overnight. All my performing experiences are refined into that 12-minute piece of theater.

(There is a knock on the door, and the stage manager tells Mr. King that the music director is out of the next show and will be replaced by a substitute. Then, there is an announcement on the intercom: "Cast and production staff, this is your half-hour call.")

Sammy: I'll put on my makeup while we talk.

Writer: Talk about the first time you were ever on stage; was it with Francisco?

Sammy: No, I wasn't doing ventriloquism yet. I was very young and very shy.

Writer: Are you still?

Sammy: Young, no. Shy, yes. Not on stage, but during the other 23 hours of the day if I'm in public.

(The interview was interrupted suddenly by a knock on the door. "Five minutes, Mr. King." He apologized and excused himself to dress and pre-set for the upcoming escorting to the stage.)

Appendix D: Francisco's Character and Script

Francisco Gonzales Garcia de la Garza Gomez Jones (pronounced Ho-nez), aka Francis Cojones, went through quite a few character changes before finding his own accented way of speaking. The first was 10 years before the actual puppet's character was created. When I was 12 years old and living at Snakeville, my grandfather's wild animal zoo, I had a Mexican-Indian friend my age named Domingo Rivas. Domingo was the barefooted son of a rattlesnake catcher, and he spoke little-to-no English. He had dark skin and dark hair that was also long and thick. Between his two very white front teeth, he had a wide space, and I often thought he could eat spaghetti with his teeth clenched by simply slurping it through the hole. I called him by his given name, Domingo, but, when talking to others about him, I called him by the nickname I had given him, "Sunday Two-Teeth." I began imitating his limited English, though mine was a colloquial American version with a slight south Texas twang. Domingo and I spent a lot of time together catching scaly tree lizards and horned toads, which were abundant in the Brownsville mesquite wooded areas, and for which we were paid 2½ cents each, or two for a nickel. Large male lizards had blue chests, and I called them "blue bellies," which Domingo, for some reason, mispronounced as "blue jellies." It made me laugh every time he saw one and shouted out "blue jelly." Our friendship lasted a few years until his family moved away, but, by then, I already had a repertoire of English words with a Spanish, "Domingo-flavored" accent.

The second character that influenced Francisco's accent came from watching *The Cisco Kid* and listening to his side companion, Pancho, played by actor Leo Carrillo. Similarly, the third influence was the phrase, "We ain't got no badges. We don't need no badges! I don't have to show you any stinkin' badges!" uttered by the Mexican bandit, Alfonso Bedoya, in the film, *Treasure of the Sierra Madre*. That phrase seemed to get a lot of imitation by everyone, though I thought most were incorrectly over-doing the accent. In the 1950s, "Speedy Gonzales," the cartoon character voiced by Mel Blanc, was a big influence, but I always liked his cousin, "Slowpoke Rodriguez," even better, though both were more of stereotypical Mexican accents.

Also in the 1950s, when *I Love Lucy* was a popular television show, Francisco's accent was more Cuban like Desi Arnaz's Ricky Ricardo role. I learned that word play and mispronunciation was funny in sitcom scripts from Lucy's imitation of Ricky's heavily-accented character. Years later, when I played Miami Beach hotels, I could hear sporadic laughter in the showrooms from Cuban waiters and busboys at Francisco's many Cuban slang expressions.

By the time I was actually working with Francisco on stage in the early 1960s, Steve Allen had a show that featured a "man on the street" sketch. Among the cast were one-time ventriloquist, Don Knotts; the very funny, but subtle, Louis Nye; and comedian, Bill Dana, who was a big hit with his Latin character, Jose Jimenez. Bill was not Mexican, or even Latino, but he was successful enough to get his own TV show, so Bill and Francisco's accents sounded a lot alike. Also, in the 1960s, Cheech Marin of Cheech & Chong, an East L.A. Mexican-American pothead, spoke in an accent that Francisco seemed to emulate whenever "we" worked in the Los Angeles area.

Additionally, there was Freddie Prinze, whose "New-Yorkican" character was converted into the TV show, *Chico and the Man*. Freddie and I had done a show together at the Friars Club in New York City, and, while I thought he was indeed a very funny young and talented comedian, his accent was far from actual Mexican-American.

Francisco finally got his own groove from a trip I once took to a Texas beach near Galveston on the Gulf of Mexico. There was a large family of Mexican-Americans having a beach party, and the father, seeing one of his sons wading into the waves alone, shouted out, "Junior, getta guay frong de wadder. Jew can no eswim and jew gonna drown." Afterwards, Francisco spoke that same way for the next 40 years with the Tex-Mex accent, but, then, he spoke more Spanish in the act when I did a four-month run at the Centro Acapulco in Acapulco, Mexico. It was there that the Mexican President asked me if I was from Northern Mexico, which was indeed complimentary to the son of a Russian Jew. Francisco's script for that show had added a lot of extra lines containing Mexican slang; obviously convincing everyone that he (I) was Mexican. And, I did the same act again when I performed for a few months in a copy of the Crazy Horse show in Mexico City's Polanco district. I also played a few weeks in Palma de Mallorca, Spain, where Francisco's Mexican accent was not welcomed as correct Spanish, which it wasn't; so that, in itself, was somewhat of a compliment.

Once Francisco's character was established in the act, it was far more important for American audiences to understand what was being said, so Francisco dropped much of the accent, which brought even bigger laughs to the gags. This was especially necessary with the distant voice when he "spoke" from under his covered cage. The following is my "family-friendly" script for Francisco's act, which has never been recorded...

Francisco, the Mexican Parrot, Script
Family-Friendly Version
(Note: S=Sammy and F=Francisco)

Introduction *(when performed after another bit or act)*

S: This next character has been performing on stages all over the world, more than 25,000 times. He is a Mexican parrot with quite a vocabulary. *(present Francisco and wait for audience reaction)* Let's see if he's in the mood to talk for us. **Parrots** can be either stubborn or on the shy side on stage. *(say to Francisco)* Would you **introduce** yourself to the audience, please. *(no response)* Uh... *(nudge and whisper)* Excuse me....

F: *(shouting)* JES!!!

S: *(reacting to shout and signaling "shhh" with finger and then pointing to microphone)* Please, don't shout; there is a microphone right here.... Everyone can hear you. *(Francisco. examines microphone)* Would you quietly...introduce yourself?

F: INTRODUCE?? *(questioning with Mexican accent "een-tro-doo-seh"??)*

S: Tell them who you are.

F: Who I are?

S: Who I AM!

F: Who JEW are?

S: Just say..."I am"...so and so.

F: Jew are a so and so.

S: Please...say your **name**.

F: Francisco Gonzales Garcia de la Garza Gomez Jones.

S: Jones?

F: Jes...ees pronounced HONEZ. Francisco Hoeness.

S: You **are** a Mexican parrot.

F: Si, **I are**...(to audience) NO C.I.A.!!!

S: Look, Francisco...*(turns and looks at S)*...we are here at _____ to entertain THIS audience.

F: *(scanning audience)* Good LUCK.

S: What would you like to do for them...sing a song....tell a joke....

F: Jew wanna hear a good choke? (joke)

S: Sure.

F: *(gagging and choking, then pauses...)* that's my choke.

S: Why don't you sing something....

F: I no sing, noh-sing.

S: You won't sing...why not?

F: Ronco de la garganta.

S: What's that mean in English?

F: I gotta sore throat. *(doing double take to "laughing" audience member)* Ees no funny, lady....no, ja ja ja.

S: Well, you sound okay to me. What if I give you a little massage...

F: A what?

S: A massage, a throat massage.

F: MAH-SAH-HEH....*(to audience)* I like mah-sah-heh...

S: *(curiously while massaging Francisco)* Is that your Adam's apple?

F: No, that's your **wristwatch**.

S: **Will** you sing....**yes** or **no**?

F: I sing JES. I sing song-sing.

S: Okay, and WHAT...will you sing?

F: A song from my country.

S: A song from YOUR country.

F: Jes, but ees no a country song.

S: That's okay....and in what key will you be singing?

F: The Mexican key.

S: The Mexican key....what is that?

F: SI!!!

S: *(gesturing toward audience and music introduction)* They're all yours.

F: I don't want all of them...just the canaries....

S: Just sing the song.

F. *(music starts; Francisco does a "Mexican grito" or "aye yai yai" and sings "When Irish Eyes Are Smiling.")*

S: Hold it, wait a minute, hold it. *(timed to music break)*

F: *(to sound tech or band)* Hold it...when I say hold it.

S: What happened?

F: Well...I was singing "When Irish Eyes Are Smiling," and you said "hole it, hole it" and they don't hole it, and this lady *(to laughing lady)* goes ja ja ja....*(pause and slow take to Sammy)* That's what happened.

S: I THOUGHT you were going to sing a Spanish song.

F: You TAWT I was going to sing a Espanich song.

S: A Spanish SONG.

F: *(mimicing)* ESPANICH ESONG.

S: *(correcting)* SPANISH.

F: ESONG!!!

S: Seems odd, can't you say "Spanish?" *(Sammy touches Francisco's feet)*

F: Yes, but don't touch my feet.

S: *(suddenly taking hand away)* Sorry.

F: I don't like you touch my feet.

S: I won't touch your feet. Now look... *(Francisco turns and looks)*...I know a little Spanish song that we could sing for this audience if you like.

F: If I like this audience, I sing. If I no like, I no sing noh-sing.

S: Well, if I sing the song, could you translate it for the audience?

F: Chure.

S: I'll take that as a yes. Okay, I'll start.

F: Jew esart.

S: I WILL START. *(firm and clear)*

F: HIT IT!!I!...Get down, get funky, oh yeah...

S: Just let me have the last word here.

F: Jew got it!!! *(to sound tech or band)* Hole it when I say hole it!!!

S: *(to audience)* The song we're going to sing for you is a traditional Mexican folk song dating back to the days of Pancho Villa and the revolution...

F: Last night, I had a date with a chicken.

S: *(series of reaction takes)* A chicken has nothing to do with the song we're going to sing.

F: No...but, it was a good chicken....FINGER licken' good. Extra CRISPY.

S: I didn't even know that parrots and chickens could...*(holding Francisco's foot)*

F: Oh yeah, we do. *(pause)* But, don't touch my feet.

(MUSIC CUE FOR "LA CUCARACHA.")

S: *(singing)* "La Cucaracha," etc.

IF NOT SUNG, A SPOKEN TRANSLATION OF THE LYRICS

F: This is the sad love story of two cockroaches.

S: TWO cockroaches?

F: Jes, jew can NO have a love estuary with only ONE cockroach.

S: True.

F: They lived together under the refrigerator of a Mexican Soul Food restaurant.

S: A Mexican Soul Food restaurant?

F: It's call Nacho Mama.

S: I can't imagine Mexican Soul Food.

F: Oh yeah, try the Chimi Changa Chitlin's...Their love was doomed from the start. *(sadly)* They could no have little baby cockroaches....

S: Why?

F: They were both boy cockroaches.

S: Proceed.

F: Then came Suzy.

S: Suzy?

F: Suzy Cockroach.

S: Suzy Cockroach?

F: She was from the wrong side of the kitchen. She was a how you say Masaje *(MAH-SAH-HEY)*.

S: Massage...oh, she was a masseuse.

F: With her feet.

S: A foot massage is very therapeutic.

F: Cockroaches have 6 feet. So, one of the other cockroaches was falling in love with her.

S: He was falling in love with Suzy. *(touching F. 's feet)*

F: Yes, but don't touch my feet.

S: So, he was falling in love with Suzy and...

F: He takes her out in the moon light and he says to her, "Oh Suzy, what's a dirty Cockroach like you doing in a nice clean place like this?"

(CUE MUSIC EXIT FRANCISCO TO CAGE.)

At this juncture, Sammy talks of starting out as a guitar player before Francisco. Options to the guitar would be any other musical instrument, or anything from 2 ukulele chords, a magic trick, an a cappella aria, a yo-yo, trick, etc. It is only a vehicle for interruption, and Francisco's Act II Entrance.

S: Sometimes getting a parrot to talk on stage is not as difficult as getting him to STOP talking. Anyway, before I got into ventriloquism I was _____. So, I'm going to perform my finest piece of work for you.

F: *(distant voice from under covered cage)* Good Luck.

S: *(long slow take to Francisco)* Thank you. *(double take)* Please don't say anything.

F: I no say no-sing...I no say no-sing, I no-sing no-sing...no sing, no sing, no sing.

S: Good night...Francisco.

F: Good night, Gringo. *(as Sammy is about to "play")* What are you going to play? *(or "do")*

S: A flamenco piece *(or option)*. Is that okay with you?

F: Jes...but, I don't like it.

S: Just don't say anything.

F: Don't touch my feet.

S: I wasn't touching your feet.

F: I wasn't talking to you.

S: *(long slow pause)* Aren't you alone in there?

F: No, I got Suzy Cockroach here. I'm going to get a foot massage.

S: Look, this is difficult.

F: This is impossible.

S: Nothing is impossible.

F: A parrot and a cockroach? Oh Suzy, touch my feet.

S: That's it, he's not going to let me do this…

(CUE MUSIC AND BOW.)

EXIT

Afterword

Dear Reader,

When I reflect on my career, the only thing that comes to mind is gratitude for my almost 60 years of having the opportunity to entertain people by doing the thing I love most in my life: walking out on stage and challenging myself time after time through the art of ventriloquism. The fact that I performed more than 26,000 shows is amazing, to be sure, but it wasn't anything I ever planned (*I'm not that clever*). My entire stage history was an evolution that simply happened. It seems to me that I was always at the right place at the right time, and I was very lucky. But, then again, was it luck, timing, or all part of a divine plan? After all, it's like the old joke: "Want to make God laugh? Tell Him your plans."

Starting with my first paid gig back in the early 1950s, all I did was practice a lot; then, go out and have fun on stage. The "business of show" was more of a mission, and, over the years, I just continued to follow my footsteps to and from the stage – my *Time on the Boards*. To me, success was always measured by my last show and my ambition for the next one. It was a blessing to take that bow at the end of each performance and hear the applause. Looking back, (something I don't often do), I have to say that, with very few exceptions, every performance was truly FUN, and maybe that's the secret of my success. All I know is that my dreams came true, along with some of the nightmares.

Could I have done more with my career? Well, that was never really a desire of mine. For whatever reason, I always cherished my privacy, so the journey I took had many side roads that kept me from wanting fame and fortune. I never liked being celebrated for my talent as I never felt worthy of my gift. A well-known agent once said of me, "Sammy King will be successful in spite of himself." I guess he was right.

I have always respected the great ventriloquists, magicians, jugglers, musicians, and variety artists that I met along the way for the amount of time they spent honing their craft, something only another artist can really understand. I feel so honored to be thought of as one of them, and it is truly a wonderful memory to have crossed paths with each of them during my lifetime.

I leave you with my simple message of realization: to waste the gift of talent is the saddest thing in the world. To be able to bring joy to others by entertaining them and giving them a distraction from everyday stress is all part of a much bigger picture. So, to the thousands of people I entertained all over the world, I say it was my pleasure; to have been paid to do what I love still amazes me; and to those of you who inspired me to follow the right path (you know who you are), I feel grateful that you came into my life.

I thank all those who are a part of ventriloquism, as a fan or a vocation. To the more than 50 ventriloquists I have mentored, inspired, or coached; it has given me so much pleasure to have been a part of your lives. So, I'll close this story with my "Golden Rule," by which I have always lived my life: "Be kind to one another and try to be one of a kind." And, finally, to borrow a phrase from a cherished friend, "If they told me I would die tomorrow...I could live with that."

**Design & Layout
by**

Made in the USA
San Bernardino, CA
21 September 2015